FRANKLIN LAKES PUBLIC LIBRARY

470 DEKORTE DRIVE

FRANKLIN LAKES, NJ 07417

(201) 891-2224

www.franklinlakeslibrary.org

Essays After Eighty

Books by Donald Hall

Essays After Eighty

DONALD HALL

Houghton Mifflin Harcourt

BOSTON   NEW YORK

For information about permission to reproduce selections from this book,
write to Permissions, Houghton Mifflin Harcourt Publishing Company,
215 Park Avenue South, New York, New York 10003.

www.hmhco.com

Library of Congress Cataloging-in-Publication Data
Hall, Donald, date, author.
[Essays. Selections]
Essays After Eighty / Donald Hall.
pages cm
ISBN 978-0-544-28704-4 (hardback)
I. Title.
PS3515.A3152A6 2014
814'.54 — dc23   2014016310

Printed in the United States of America
DOC 10 9 8 7 6 5 4

The following essays previously appeared elsewhere: "One Road" and
"Remains" in *The American Scholar;* "A Yeti in the District" in *New Letters;* "Out
the Window" in *The New Yorker;* "Thank You Thank You," "Three Beards," and
"Garlic with Everything" in *The New Yorker*'s "Page-Turner"; "No Smoking,"
"Physical Malfitness," and "Death" in *Playboy;* "Essays After Eighty" in *Slice.*

Jane Kenyon, "The First Eight Days of the Beard" from *Collected Poems.*
Copyright © 2005 by The Estate of Jane Kenyon. Reprinted with the
permission of The Permissions Company, Inc.,
on behalf of Graywolf Press, www.graywolfpress.org.

Donald Hall, "Ardor" from *The Painted Bed.* Copyright © 2002 by
Houghton Mifflin Company. Reprinted with the permission of
Houghton Mifflin Harcourt Publishing Company.

For
Andrew, Philippa, Emily, Allison,
Ariana, Abigail, and Peter

Contents

Essays After Eighty

Out the Window

TODAY IT IS JANUARY, mid-month, midday, and mid–New Hampshire. I sit in my blue armchair looking out the window. I teeter when I walk, I no longer drive, I look out the window. Snow started before I woke, and by now it looks to be ten inches; they say we might have a foot and a half. There are three windows beside me where I sit, the middle one deep and wide. Outside is a narrow porch that provides shade in the summer, in winter a barrier against drifts. I look at the barn forty yards away, which heaves like a frigate in a gale. I watch birds come to my feeder, hanging from a clapboard in my line of sight. All winter, juncos and chickadees take nourishment here. When snow is as thick as today, the feeder bends under the weight of a dozen birds at once. They swerve from their tree perches, peck, and fly back to bare branches. Prettily they light, snap beaks into seed, and burst away: nuthatches, evening grosbeaks, American goldfinches, sparrows.

Most days, squirrels pilfer from the birds. I'm happy to feed the squirrels — tree rats with the agility of point guards — but in fair weather they frighten my finches. They leap from snowbank to porch to feeder, and gobble my chickadee feed. They hang on to a rusty horseshoe, permanently nailed to the doorjamb by my grandparents, which provides a toehold for their elongated bodies. Their weight tilts the feeder sideways, scaring away the flightier birds while the bravest continue to peck at a careening table. No squirrels today. In thick snow, they hide in tunnels under snowdrifts, and a gaggle of birds feed at the same time.

As daylight weakens, snow persists. In the twilight of four p.m., the birds have gone, sleeping somewhere somehow. No: a nuthatch lands for a last seed. The cow barn raises its dim shape. It was built in 1865, and I gaze at it every day of the year. A few years ago, when we had an especially snowy winter, I thought I would lose the barn. A yard of whiteness rose on the old shingles, and I could find no one to clear it off. The roof was frail and its angles dangerously steep. Finally friends came up with friends who shoveled it, despite its precariousness, and the following summer I hired a roofer to nail metal over the shingles. Shingle-colored tin disposes of snow by sliding it off. Now I look at the sharp roof of the carriage shed at the barn's front, where a foot of snow has accumulated. The lower two-thirds has fallen onto drifts below. The snow at the shed's metal top, irregular as the cliff of a glacier, looks ready to slide down. In the bluing air of afternoon, it is vanilla icing that tops an enormous cake. A Brobdingnagian hand will scrape it off.

Suddenly I hear a crash, as the snowplow strikes the end of my driveway. High in the cab sits my cousin Steve, who expertly backs and lurches forward, backs and lurches forward. The driveway is oval, with Route 4 flattening one end, and Steve executes the top curve with small motions of snow-budging, building great drifts back far enough from the driveway so that there's room for cars — and for Steve to pack away more snow when he needs to. It's his first visit for this snowstorm, and his plowing is incomplete. He will return with exact skill in the middle of the night, when the snow stops, and tidy the path among the drifts. When he thuds into the driveway at three a.m., I will hear him in my sleep and wake for a moment, taking pleasure from Steve's attack on drifts in the black night.

My mother turned ninety in the Connecticut house where she had lived for almost sixty years, and spent her last decade looking out the window. (My father died at fifty-two.) For my mother's birthday, my wife Jane Kenyon and I arrived at her house early, and at noon my children and grandchildren surprised Gramma Lucy with a visit. We hugged and laughed together, taking pictures, until I watched my mother's gaiety collapse into exhaustion. I shooed the young ones away, and my mother leaned back in her familiar Barcalounger, closing her eyes until strength returned. A few months later she had one of her attacks of congestive heart failure, only a week after her most recent. An ambulance took her to Yale–New Haven Hospital. Jane and I drove down from New Hampshire to care for her when she came home. She told us, "I tried not to dial 911." She knew she could no longer live alone, her pleasure and her pride. We moved her to a facility attached to a hospital near us in New Hampshire.

She died a month short of ninety-one. Her brain was still good. A week before she died, she read *My Ántonia* for the tenth time. Willa Cather had always been a favorite. Most of the time in old age she read Agatha Christie. She said that one of the advantages of being ninety was that she could read a detective story again, only two weeks after she first read it, without any notion of which character was the villain. Even so, her last months were mostly bleak. Her arthritic knees kept her to bed and chair, and the food was terrible. We visited every day until she died. A year later, Jane, at forty-seven, was dying of leukemia, and showed me poems she had been working on before she took sick. One was "In the Nursing Home," about my mother at the end. Jane used the image of a horse running in wide circles, the circles growing smaller until they ceased.

Twenty years later, my circles narrow. Each season, my balance gets worse, and sometimes I fall. I no longer cook for myself but microwave widower food, mostly Stouffer's. My fingers are clumsy and slow with buttons. This winter I wear warm pullover shirts; my mother spent her last decade in caftans. For years I drove slowly and cautiously, but when I was eighty I had two accidents. I stopped driving before I killed somebody, and now when I shop or see a doctor, someone has to drive me. If I fly to do a poetry reading, my dear companion Linda Kunhardt, who lives an hour away, must wheelchair me through airport and security. I read my poems sitting down. If I want to look at paintings, Linda wheelchairs me through museums. New poems no longer come to me, with their prodigies of metaphor and assonance. Prose endures. I feel the circles grow smaller, and old age is a ceremony of losses, which is on the whole preferable to dying at forty-seven or fifty-two. When I lament and darken over my diminishments, I accomplish nothing. It's better to sit at the window all day, pleased to watch birds, barns, and flowers. It is a pleasure to write about what I do.

Generation after generation, my family's old people sat at this window to watch the year. There are beds in this house where babies were born, where the same babies died eighty years later. My grandmother Kate lived to be ninety-seven. Kate's daughter, my mother, owed her "early" death to two packs a day — unfiltered Chesterfields first, then filtered Kents. My mother was grateful to cigarettes; they allowed her to avoid dementia. Before senescence my grandmother looked out the window at Mount Kearsarge, five miles to the south. As I gaze in the same direction, I see only a triangle of foothill, because softwood has grown so tall that it gets in the way. When Kate was a child here, elms blocked the foothill. They grew tall on both sides of Route 4, some of them high enough to meet over the center of the road. When she was ninety-four, she stumbled on the porch outside the window. Her fractured shin put her in the hospital — Kate, who had never taken to bed except to bear children. Her hospital stay affected her mind. Three years later, in the Peabody Home, I sat beside her listening to Cheyne-Stokes breathing. I was holding her hand when she died.

After months of snow and snowbirds, I look out the window at flowers and a luxury of green leaves and always at the wooden ancient hill of the barn. For the last ten years in her house, my mother sat in her chair looking out a window, but she did not see what I see. She was born in this New Hampshire farmhouse, growing up when the barn was heavy with Holsteins, but turned old in my father's territory, on a street corner in the suburb of Hamden, Connecticut. She looked not at a barn but at other six-room houses built in the twenties. Twice a day she watched children walk by with their backpacks, ambling to school in the morning, returning in the afternoon. They attended Spring Glen Elementary School on Whitney Avenue, to which I had trudged for eight years when it was Spring Glen Grammar School. Midday in winter, she watched it snow, and watched the Connecticut birds, cousins to New Hampshire's, fly to the feeder outside her window.

With aching knees she hobbled to the kitchen to warm up canned clam chowder. From April through September, sitting by her window at night, she listened to WTIC from Hartford, carrying Boston Red Sox games. In middle age she had been a substitute teacher, and she was proud that a Red Sox broadcaster had been her pupil. Her father, in New Hampshire, followed the Red Sox by reading the *Boston Post*, which arrived two days after the games. My mother heard baseball as it happened, from the small radio beneath her ear, next to the ashtray. (In another room, an enormous steam-powered television showed a continual blank screen; she did not want to move from her chair.) The radio games replaced her window of schoolchildren and birds. During the months between baseball seasons she spent her nights reading *Reader's Digest*, Henry David Thoreau, *Time*, Robert Frost — and Agatha Christie.

My summer nights are NESN and the Boston Red Sox.

When I was a child, I loved old people. My New Hampshire grandfather was my model human being. He wasn't old. He was in his sixties and early seventies when I hayed with him, only seventy-seven when he died, but of course I thought he was old. He was a one-horse farmer — Riley was his horse — with an old-fashioned multiple farm. He raised cattle and sheep and chickens, with hives for bees and a sugarhouse for boiling sap into maple syrup. He worked every day all year, mostly from five a.m. to seven or eight at night — milking, lambing, fencing, logging, spreading manure, planting, weeding, haying, harvesting, each night locking up chickens against foxes. Summers I helped with farm work and listened to him reminisce. All year he walked rapidly from one task to another, in his good nature smiling a private half smile as he remembered stories, or recited to himself the poems he had memorized for school.

After a life of loving the old, by natural law I turned old myself. Decades followed each other — thirty was terrifying, forty I never noticed because I was drunk, fifty was best with a total change of life, sixty began to extend the bliss of fifty — and then came my cancers, Jane's death, and over the years I traveled to another universe. However alert we are, however much we think we know what will happen, antiquity remains an unknown, unanticipated galaxy. It is alien, and old people are a separate form of life. They have green skin, with two heads that sprout antennae. They can be pleasant, they can be annoying — in the supermarket, these old ladies won't get out of my way — but most important they are permanently other. When we turn eighty, we understand that we are extraterrestrial. If we forget for a moment that we are old, we are reminded when we try to stand up, or when we encounter someone young, who appears to observe green skin, extra heads, and protuberances.

People's response to our separateness can be callous, can be goodhearted, and is always condescending. When a woman writes to the newspaper, approving of something I have done, she calls me "a nice old gentleman." She intends to praise me, with "nice" and "gentleman." "Old" is true enough, and she lets us know that I am not a grumpy old fart, but "nice" and "gentleman" put me in a box where she can rub my head and hear me purr. Or maybe she would prefer me to wag my tail, lick her hand, and make ingratiating dog noises. At a family dinner, my children and grandchildren pay fond attention to me; I may be peripheral, but I am not invisible. A grandchild's college roommate, encountered for the first time, pulls a chair to sit with her back directly in front of me, cutting me off from the family circle: I don't exist.

When kindness to the old is condescending, it is aware of itself as benignity while it asserts its power. Sometimes the reaction to antiquity becomes farce. I go to Washington to receive the National Medal of Arts and arrive two days early to look at paintings. At the National Gallery of Art, Linda pushes me in a wheelchair from painting to painting. We stop by a Henry Moore carving. A museum guard, a man in his sixties with a small pepper-and-salt mustache, approaches us and helpfully tells us the name of the sculptor. I wrote a book about Moore and knew him well. Linda and I separately think of mentioning my connection but instantly suppress the notion — egotistic, and maybe embarrassing to the guard. A couple of hours later, we emerge from the cafeteria and see the same man, who asks Linda if she enjoyed her lunch. Then he bends over to address me, wags his finger, smiles a grotesque smile, and raises his voice to ask, "Did we have a nice din-din?"

In spring when the feeder is down, stowed away in the toolshed until October, I watch the fat robins come back, blue jays that harass them, warblers, red-winged blackbirds, thrushes, orioles. Mourning doves crouch in the grass, nibbling seeds. A robin returns every year to refurbish her nest after the wintry ravage. She adds new straw, twigs, and lint. Soon enough she lays eggs, sets on them with short excursions for food, then tends to three or four small beaks that open for her scavenging. Before long, the infants stand, spread and clench their wings, peer at their surroundings, and fly away. I cherish them, and look for farther nests, small clots in branches of oak or Norway maple visible from my window. The blackest crows peck through my grass. Most strange and wonderful are the hummingbirds that helicopter by the porch, wings blurred with incessant whirring. They jab into the horns of hollyhocks, gobble some sweet, and zig off to zag back again for another taste.

Late March or April onward, depending on the year, I watch the flowers erupt and subside. Snowdrops crack the wintry earth, crocuses, and dazzling daffodils. Tulips rise in extravagant crimsons and golds, metallic fleshy shapes that ask to be filled. In June, peonies bloom at the edge of my porch, a column of them, as their buds swell green until they burst into white and feathery soccer balls—and then a thunderstorm shatters the blossoms. There are lilies of the valley and, across the yard, a patch of old single roses that some years are few and some years put forth a hundred blossoms — first white ones, then pink, then red, lofting beside the road's gutter as two centuries ago they rose beside a trail for oxen.

One day, I look out the window to see great machines at work. A farmer neighbor comes to harvest the grass that has grown dark and thick in my fields. The first contraption cuts the hay. Another rakes it, and another shapes it into huge circular bales, which a last machine lifts with great clamps onto a truck that replaces the old hayrack. My neighbor collects for his cows in winter, and returns a second time and a third as new grass rises. I watch out the window. These are the fields where my grandfather and I, seventy years ago, cut hay with a horse-drawn mower, trimmed the shaggy edges by hand with scythes, pitched it onto a horse-drawn hayrack, and stacked it in high lofts of the barn. Cow manure, spread on the fields in April, fed the grass for a century and a half. Decades after my grandfather died, the goodness wore out, exposing New Hampshire's sandy soil. My neighbor spreads lime late in spring.

Flowers by turn rise and fall all summer — foxglove, sweet alyssum, bee balm. I watch two wild turkeys gobble as they strut stiffly up the slope toward the barn. Behind them four small offspring hurry to keep up. Daylilies ascend the hill beyond them, the same bright orange wildflowers that grow in ditches and in clearings beside cellar holes. Indian paintbrush raise late flags. Cornflowers bloom, and leaves of swamp maples flare the first reds of autumn.

Whatever the season, I watch the barn. I see it through this snow in January, and in August I will gaze at trailing vines of roses on a trellis against the vertical boards. I watch at the height of summer and when darkness comes early in November. From my chair I look at the west side, a gorgeous amber laved by the setting sun, as rich to the eyes as the darkening sweet of bees' honey. The unpainted boards are dark at the bottom, and rise toward the top in a brownish yellow that holds light the longest. At barn's end is the horse's window, where Riley stuck out his head to count the pickups and Fords on Route 4. I study the angles of roof, a geometry of tilting, symmetrical and importantly asymmetrical, endlessly losing and recapturing itself. Over eighty years, it has changed from a working barn to a barn for looking at. Down the road, I see the ghosts of elm trees, which lined the road when Route 4 led to the Grafton Turnpike. A hundred and fifty years transformed them from green shoots to blighted bark. Out the window, I watch a white landscape that turns pale green, dark green, yellow and red, brown under bare branches, until snow falls again.

Essays After Eighty

STARTING IN THE seventh grade I wrote lines of poetry, poetry, poetry. After two books of poems, I wrote *String Too Short
to Be Saved,* about childhood summers on my grandparents'
New Hampshire farm. I wrote in paragraphs, not in lines, in order to tell family stories.

Poems are image-bursts from brain-depths, words flavored by
buttery long vowels. As I grew older — collapsing into my seventies, glimpsing ahead the cliffs of the eighties, colliding into
eighty-five — poetry abandoned me. How could I complain after
seventy years of diphthongs? The sound of poems is sensual,
even sexual. The shadow mind pours out metaphors — at first
poets may not understand what they say — that lead to emotional
revelation. For a male poet, imagination and tongue-sweetness
require a blast of hormones. When testosterone diminishes . . .

My last book of poems came out. Writing paragraphs, I looked
out the window and wrote about what I saw. Snow was falling,
later daffodils were bursting. I luxuriated in the paragraph, the

sentence, varieties of fast and slow, rise and fall — improvising toward a final fullness.

The greatest pleasure in writing is rewriting. My early drafts are always wretched. At first a general verb like "move" is qualified by the adverb "quickly." After sixty tries I come up with a particular, possibly witty verb and drop the adverb. Originally I wrote "poetry suddenly left me," which after twelve drafts became "poetry abandoned me" — with another sentence to avoid self-pity. When my doctor told me I had diabetes, I was incredulous. I said, "You mean I am pre-diabetic." Writing in this book, I changed a verb to mock my silly presumption. "'You mean I am pre-diabetic,' I explained."

Revision takes time, a pleasing long process. Some of these essays took more than eighty drafts, some as few as thirty. Writing prose, I used to be a bit quicker. Maybe I discovered more things to be persnickety about. More likely age has slowed down my access to the right word. Because of multiple drafts I have been accused of self-discipline. Really I am self-indulgent, I cherish revising so much.

Once I worked with William Shawn, editor of the *New Yorker* from 1952 to 1987, who is well remembered for his fastidious scrutiny of sentences, his polite and fierce insistence on repair. First from the magazine I would receive galleys of text with suggestions or requests for changes, maybe a hundred each galley. When the pages of the corrected version arrived, there were thirty more queries on each. A week before publication, my telephone rang at six p.m. "Do you have time, Mr. Hall, to go over your essay? It might take a few hours." "Go ahead, Mr. Shawn." "In the first sentence we have found a serial comma we think we might with profit remove."

As I work over clauses and commas, I understand that rhythm and cadence have little connection to import, but they should carry the reader on a pleasurable journey. Sentences can be long, three or more complete clauses dancing together, or two clauses with one leaning on the other, or an added phrase of only a few syllables. Sentences and paragraphs are as various as human beings. I like the effect — see John McPhee — of a paragraph three pages long, glued together by transitions that never sound like transitions.

After a three-page paragraph, maybe a one-line blurt.

There are problems in writing one can learn to avoid. Almost always, in my poems or essays, the end goes on too long. "In case you don't get it, this is what I just said." Cut it out. Let the words flash a conclusion, then get out of the way. Sometimes the writer intrudes — me, myself, and I — between the reader and the page. Don't begin paragraphs with "I." For that matter, try not to begin sentences with the personal pronoun. Avoid "me" and "my" when you can. Writing memoir, don't say, "I remember that in my childhood nothing happened to me." Say, "In childhood nothing happened."

Nevertheless, for seventy-odd years I have been writing about myself, which has led to a familiar scene: I meet someone, we chat, something stirs my memory, I begin to tell an anecdote — and the head in front of me nods up and down and smiles. She knows this story because I have put it in print, possibly three times.

Avoid the personal pronoun when you can — but not the personal. My first book of poems said "I," but the word was distant, a stiff and poetic "I." In my best poems and prose I've become steadily more naked, with a nakedness that disguises itself by wearing clothes. A scrupulous passion of style — word choice, syntax, punctuation, order, rhythm, specificity — sets forth not only the writer's rendering of barns and hollyhocks, but the writer's feelings and counterfeelings.

Essays, like poems and stories and novels, marry heaven and hell. Contradiction is the cellular structure of life. Sometimes north dominates, sometimes south — but if the essay doesn't include contraries, however small they be, the essay fails. When I looked out the window taking joy in sparrows, snow, Mount Kearsarge, lilacs, and wild turkeys, my essay was incomplete. It required contrast, required something nasty or ridiculous. Happily I found it. When "Out the Window" appeared in print a hundred letters arrived. Terry Gross interviewed me for *Fresh Air*. Almost everyone paid as much attention to a goon's baby talk as to the landscape. I thank a museum guard at the National Gallery.

A Yeti in the District

VISITS TO WASHINGTON have punctuated my life. I watched a victory parade in 1945. My last trip was the most memorable, early in March 2011, when I received the National Medal of Arts. Linda and I went down two days early to look at paintings and sculpture — mostly the National Gallery, the Hirshhorn, and the Phillips. I can't stand long, so Linda has pushed me in a wheelchair through the thousand museums. On the day of the medal, she wheeled me from the Willard InterContinental Hotel to the White House. Waiting at the entrance to go through security, I looked up to see Philip Roth, whom I recognized from long ago. I loved his novels. He saw me in the hotel's wheelchair — my enormous beard and erupting hair, my body wracked with antiquity — and said, "I haven't seen you for fifty years!" How did he remember me? We had met in George Plimpton's living room in the 1950s. I praised what he wrote about George in *Exit Ghost.* He seemed pleased, and glanced down at me in the chair. "How are *you* doing?" I told him fine, "I'm still writing."

He said, "What else is there?"

• • •

In 1945, when I was sixteen, I took the train to the old Union Station, District of Columbia, where my Exeter friend Ted Lewis picked me up. The railroad station was a lofty cement cathedral, like city depots everywhere before airplanes took over. Ted drove us to the family flat in Alexandria, where I met his parents and his younger brother Jay. Ted Lewis Sr. wrote a Washington column for the *New York Daily News,* an old liberal serving up conservative opinions for his bosses. He was cynical, sharp, and funny. For a week my friend and I talked and drove around. He brought me to a Saturday-night YMCA dance, where I flirted with a pretty girl not quite sixteen. She told me she was a Methodist. Cocky and a year older, I condescended to tell her about Dr. Method and Mr. Ist, of whom she had not heard. Ted showed me the District, taking me to the Lincoln and the Jefferson memorials, and to Washington's penis on the Mall. We never looked into the National Gallery or the Library of Congress or the White House. One thing we did no one would ever do again. Ted and Jay and I stood at the edge of Pennsylvania Avenue for Eisenhower's homecoming parade. Not long after V-E Day (not long before V-J Day) the general rode past us standing upright in the back of a convertible with his arms arced over his head in the victory sign. We cheered him, celebrating the end of a long and murderous war. None of us voted for Ike when he ran for President. None of us forgot the parade.

My next trip to the District of Columbia was twenty-four years later, November 15, 1969, in the company of my teenage son Andrew. From Ann Arbor, where I taught, we rode all night on a bus to march against the Vietnam War and President Nixon — before Watergate, before the resignation. I don't remember much of our demonstration except for the hordes alighting from buses, mostly from college campuses, to parade with honorable, noisy enthusiasm. In those days we wore long hair whether we were fifteen or forty-one. I remember passing the Justice Department, delighting in the notion that John and Martha Mitchell were quaking above us. On the telephone I had told Ted Lewis what Andrew and I were doing; he and his father asked us to the National Press Club for lunch. Privileged, at midday we edged from the multitude and entered the dining room where our friends were waiting. Just inside the door we saw two men at a table, and I was surprised to recognize one of them. It was Charles Waldo Bailey II, whom I had known at Exeter, a bright and supercilious boy who had become the Washington correspondent for the *Minneapolis Star Tribune*. Chuck Bailey wore a suit, as his tablemate did, as did the rest of the room. Andrew and I dangled pigtails, wearing T-shirts that attested to our politics — like our beads, like our rude buttons. When Bailey looked up from his table in response to my greeting, he was as cold as his Manhattan on the rocks. His companion glared at a glass of ginger ale. I was annoyed at Bailey, and when we joined the Lewises I spoke of his rudeness. Ted's father squinted across the room. "He's having lunch," he told us, "with Ron Ziegler." We knew the name of Nixon's press secretary.

After Ziegler left the table, doubtless to conceal plans for bombing Cambodia, Charles Waldo Bailey II walked to our table and was cordial.

• • •

I did not return until Jane and I flew to Jimmy Carter's poetry do, in January of 1980. The President himself had not yet published his book of poems, but it was known that he liked the stuff. A year before Reagan took over, the Carters decided to honor American poets. Jane and I circled the White House in a taxi looking for our entrance, and passed a bunch of tourists waiting to enter. "Look at the poets," I said, laughing, "trying to get in." When the taxi followed our directions, we joined the poets trying to get in.

The poetic crowd was huge. There must have been sixty poets, and each brought a guest. The line budged slowly through security toward its destination. I seemed to recognize the face in front of me, surely from a book jacket. Then I realized he was the best-selling poet of the era, Rod McKuen, who wrote *Listen to the Warm*. In every generation there is one poet whom high school boys read to high school girls in order to get into their pants. In my day it was Walter Benton, whose *This Is My Beloved* was endorsed by the anthologist Louis Untermeyer in publishers' ads ("I certainly do not find these poems pornographic") that swept a teenage mob into bookstores. Rod McKuen's poems didn't approach pornography — though they did approach Hallmark. The White House had asked the National Endowment for the Arts to list poets for invitation, and the original list did not include McKuen. Pressure crashed on the NEA — from furious agents and publicists, and from Congress, which controls the budget. Rod McKuen stood in line.

A dozen poets read their poems, in groups of three. Jane and I were not among the readers, so we listened to Phil Levine and his gang. Afterward we gathered to mingle, chatting and drinking white wine. I had not seen John Ashbery or Adrienne Rich for years; they had been my classmates at Harvard. We talked to my old friend Jim Wright, who walked with a cane. (Soon I saw him at Mount Sinai, then at a hospice in the Bronx, where he died.) There were Maxine Kumin, Robert Hayden, Gwendolyn Brooks, Bob Creeley, and De Snodgrass. We shook the President's hand. He greeted us all, looking in our eyes, asking where we came from. Of course he expected everybody to be a professor, but by that time I had resigned from Michigan and moved to the old family house. When I told him "New Hampshire," he said, "Dartmouth?" with a little nod of his head. I was flustered and named my hometown, "Wilmot." He said, "Oh," almost as if he remembered Wilmot State. There is not even a store in Wilmot.

The National Endowment for the Arts was established by Congress in 1965, when Lyndon Johnson was President. It gives grants to artists and to arts institutions: painters and museums, writers and publishers. Late in the 1980s, I returned to Washington for NEA panels, once to support poets with fellowships, another time to fund literary organizations. Then in 1991 I became an NEA councilor. (I took the job in order to defend obscene art from congressional attack.) I spent boring sessions in the NEA quarters at the Old Post Office, and attended the 1991 White House ceremony for the National Medal of Arts. I sat in an auditorium to observe Bush the First bestow the medals. (I had seen him before, in 1948, when I was a Harvard freshman and the World War II veteran played first base for Yale.) As Bush stood on a raised platform, I watched a Marine help the country

singer Roy Acuff climb two steps for the bestowal. I do not remember some of the honorees, but others included the painter
Richard Diebenkorn, the dancer Pearl Primus, and the violin-
ist Isaac Stern. The President said a word or two — this oilman
from Texas with a desiccated Ivy League accent — and put a be-
medaled ribbon around each neck. In the receiving line, I shook
Bush's hand. (Jane wouldn't touch my hand for a week.) We
repaired to another room for lunch. The President made mild
introductory remarks, and lunch was exemplary. During coffee,
Bush rose rapping on his water glass with a spoon. "Well," he
said, "I don't know about you artists, but I have work to do." We
murmured the required laugh. "You're all heroes of the arts, but
there are other heroes too. Fifty years ago Joe DiMaggio hit in
fifty-six straight games, and Ted Williams batted .406." He swept
his arm toward the end of the room, and we turned to see Joe
DiMaggio and Ted Williams standing in the doorway smiling.
The artist-heroes leapt in a standing ovation. Isaac Stern, short
and plump and old, thundered his palms with gusto — while
the tall men in the doorway disappeared as swiftly as they had
arrived.

In time the word spread. This afternoon the President's work
would fly him with Williams and DiMaggio to the All-Star Game
in Toronto.

In 1995 Jane died of leukemia. I grieved, I mourned, I wrote
about her. I read her poems and mine at colleges and confer-
ences. Much later I was Poet Laureate of the United States for
a year, which allowed me more of Washington's museums. The
Library of Congress was welcoming and helpful, but I was not

a productive Laureate, and resigned after one year. I returned to the District with Linda for an interview with Diane Rehm. I returned for my daughter Philippa's fiftieth birthday party.

Then, in February 2011, came a telephone call from the current director of the NEA. President Obama would award me a National Medal of Arts on March second. I would go back to the District of Columbia to be adorned, as twenty years earlier I had watched Bush the First adorn others. Recipients in 2011 included several musical sorts — Van Cliburn, James Taylor, Sonny Rollins — as well as artists and directors and biographers and institutions. Meryl Streep could not attend because she was being Margaret Thatcher in London. Ella Baff received an arts medal on behalf of Jacob's Pillow and its dancers. The National Endowment for the Humanities honored its recipients on the same occasion, and somehow included three novelists. Philip Roth had already received the arts medal, during the Clinton administration, and I was delighted to find two other literary friends — Joyce Carol Oates and Wendell Berry. I asked a humanities administrator why novelists belonged to humanities and not to art, and she told me that no one had any idea.

The night before the awards, the two endowments sponsored a huge, fatuous, black-tie dinner, I suppose an annual perk for ill-paid staffers. The high point of the evening was when the Indian filmmaker Mira Nair gave an elegant keynote address. All of us were splendidly outfitted. It was shocking to see Wendell in an immaculate rented tuxedo instead of his usual overalls. Linda had brought a long and fancy dress with a sparkly top, which cost her $37.45 at a consignment shop. My formalwear was a fifty-year-old acrylic tux, a plain white shirt, and a clip-on tie.

Next afternoon, we arrived at the White House an hour before the ceremony. Men and women in uniform gave us a brief tour of decorative rooms, then showed us the empty East Room, where we would receive our medals. Each of us sat in an assigned chair, and we rehearsed protocol — how we would climb to the platform, how we would turn toward the President, how we would return to our seats. A small Marine practiced saying our names aloud. Van Cliburn corrected a vowel. Mark di Suvero gave detailed instruction. My name was no problem. Most of us wore dark suits. Sonny Rollins wore a flowing red silk shirt and Mark di Suvero a bright red jacket. Ella Baff's shoes were equally red. I had planned to use my one remaining suit, blue silk bought in Bombay in 1993, but the pants no longer fit. My Poet Laureate outfit and my gray flannels had been perforated by moths. I wore khakis, and found a black jacket that would cover my white shirt from the night before. I added a cherished red silk necktie bought in Shanghai.

We waited next door while the guests arrived and settled in. Then we marched in order down the center aisle to take our seats up front. The band stopped, and we were applauded. Michelle Obama sat in the front row wearing a shiny green dress. The President in a grave suit entered past a table heaped with medals. He declared that this occasion was more pleasing than most of his work. He praised the centrality of art and literature, and talked of Robert Frost's visit to Russia, and of *Portnoy's Complaint*. Mostly, all I could hear was my heartbeat. When he stopped, the Marine summoned us each by name, and identified me as a former Lorit. A military man took my arm to help me climb two stairs, as I had seen another do for Roy Acuff. I told the President how much I admired him. He hugged my shoulder and bent speaking several sentences into my left ear, which is totally deaf. I heard nothing except my heart's pounding. When my friends watched on the Internet, seeing the President address me, they asked what he had said. I told them that he said either "Your work is immeasurably great" or "All your stuff is disgusting crap," but I couldn't make out which.

He draped a purple ribbon around my neck from which hung a heavy, gold-colored medal, and the soldier helped me step down. When all of us had been honored, we returned up the aisle we had descended. Nancy Pelosi sat in the crowd and I gave her a thumbs-up. We returned to the room next door, where the President and the First Lady joined us. We lined up to be photographed, first all together, then singly between our host and hostess. Each of us posed for two seconds and was replaced by the next medalist. It was a few weeks before I received the ten-by-twelve, signed (as it were) by Barack and Michelle Obama. "Thank you for years of inspiring work!" One Size Fits All. In the picture they both grin gorgeously — while I am perpetually unable to smile when posing for a photograph. I look as sour as Dick Cheney, sinking between two tall, elegant figures.

We exited into an area where we met the rest of the world. I hugged Linda, and Allison my granddaughter, who had studied art history and English at Vassar and whom I had been able to add to the guest list. I saw friends I didn't expect, and mingled with other medal wearers. We had been silent and shy. We drank some nonalcoholic liquid, and after ten minutes it was as if we had drained a dozen martinis. Everyone became loud, friendly, and jolly. I told James Taylor that we once sat on a platform together, not aware of each other's line of work. I chattered with Joyce Carol Oates and happily greeted Wendell Berry. Mark di Suvero, Ella Baff, and Van Cliburn bubbled. Sonny Rollins was quiet and the best to talk with. My son had attended his 9/11 concert, so I brought him my son's gratitude. Linda sat chatting with him about politics and literature for half an hour; they exchanged addresses and later letters. Allison moved among writers and musicians she had read and listened to. Everybody took photographs of everybody standing with everybody.

Gradually we diminished. Our exhausted party returned to the Willard. My agents took us out for dinner with the Berrys. Allison at twenty-three was carded for her glass of wine. Wendell, who sat opposite my beautiful granddaughter, insisted on being carded also, and chatted with us all. His laugh — as Jane used to say — makes the best sound in the universe. After dinner, when a taxi took my family back to the Willard, I completed my crowded day with customary aplomb. Stone sober, I fell down as I stepped out of the taxi, and a bellhop caught me midair.

Leaving Washington this time, more than sixty years after Eisenhower's parade, I returned to my New Hampshire solitude. I cherish my visits over the decades — marching against the war, Jimmy Carter's party, defending unacceptable art, honors for Isaac Stern, the apparition of baseball heroes, my daughter's fiftieth birthday, President Obama's embrace — but nothing in human life is unmixed, and honors inevitably balance themselves with self-doubt. Everyone knows that medals are rubber. During his victory parade, did Eisenhower consider that George Marshall was possibly the better general? My daughter enjoyed her birthday party, but of course she thought of another decade. A friend who won the Pulitzer told me that, if she also won the National Book Award, she would know that her work was unredeemable. In 2011 the District of Columbia sent me home feeling not only worthless but ecstatic.

The next day I got back to writing. What else was there?

Well, there was anticlimax. When Linda and I returned to my house, we found a stack of five *Concord Monitor*s, the local paper, delivered in kindness by the morning deliverer. Top of the first page was a photograph of the President looming over me, hanging the medal around my neck. My mouth is open in life's widest smile as I confront the neatly dressed Obama in my sports coat and khakis, with my frizzy hair and reckless beard. I thought it was the best photograph of my life. It must have been Alexandra Petri's favorite too, who blogs for the *Washington Post* and a day later posted the joyous picture. (She graduated from Harvard in 2010, fifty-nine years after I did.) She identified me, called me a poet, and assured her audience that I was not a yeti. She announced a contest for a caption. Entry upon entry rolled in, uniformly gormless and gleeful with ridicule. Then there were reactions. I was praised and Ms. Petri was scolded. I was defended as a poet, and flattered despite my appearance. Philip Terzian wrote a kind essay in the *Weekly Standard*—but attacked the *Washington Post* as liberal. An Alaskan eye picked it up, and

Sarah Palin blogged to defend a nameless "eighty-two-year-old cancer survivor" against the *WaPo*. Of course I enjoyed the attention, an extra scoop on my ice cream cone. With our increasing longevity, Ms. Petri should live to be a hundred. May she grow a beard.

One Road

IN DECEMBER OF 1952 my first wife Kirby and I left Vienna to drive through the Russian sector of Austria into Yugoslavia. At the border crossing, on a two-lane macadam road with no other car in sight, we stopped to present documents that permitted us to enter Marshal Tito's country. Walking back to our Morris, we met a man approaching from a big black car headed toward Austria. He looked important, like a diplomat or a capo. He had seen the initials of national origin on our small convertible, and addressed us in English. I held in my hand our confusing travel directions. We asked the man if Zagreb was straight ahead.

He shrugged and told us, "There is only one road in Yugoslavia."

It was not long after our wedding. When I finished my initial year at Oxford, I flew home to marry Kirby, who had been my girlfriend in college. We had met on a blind date. When my college roommate asked his fiancée to fix me up, she asked, "How tall is he?" Kirby was pretty, intelligent, classy, and six foot one.

I was only an inch taller, and found her height exotic. We had a good time together, sophomore and senior, and dated again, and again, and again. One thing led to another. When I spent a year at Oxford we missed each other. We wrote letters back and forth, and by mail arranged to get married.

From London I flew to New York, seventeen hours on a Lockheed Constellation with its triple tail. My return was happy and then frantic with preparation. After the September ceremony we had no time for a honeymoon. We visited my grandparents in New Hampshire — my grandfather's heart attack kept them from the wedding — then took passage to Southampton on the *Queen Elizabeth*. As a wedding present, my Connecticut grandfather Hall had ordered us an English automobile, a tiny green Morris Minor, which we were to pick up in London and, after Oxford, ship back to the United States. From the dealer's, we headed out into heavy traffic. I drove for the first time on the sinister side of the road, which was terrifying. Kirby stiffened beside me, while I concentrated to stay left until we reached Oxford and the Banbury Road flat we had rented. College terms were eight weeks long, followed by six weeks off. I spent the autumn taking notes for my B.Litt. thesis at the Bodleian, in Duke Humfrey's Library, the oldest and coldest section. Kirby had the day alone, and spent much of her time reading Trollope or exploring our neighborhood of small shops — apothecary, fishmonger, butcher. In the evening we attended Oxford's continuous party. For Kirby these gatherings were composed of strangers who did not notice her. When I had time at the flat, I attended to my poems.

• • •

By the end of term I had done my research and figured to begin my thesis when Oxford started again in January. What would we do for our six weeks' vacation? Another American gave us the answer: we should motor across Europe and down Yugoslavia to Greece and Athens. It was a simple drive, we were told, and the weather agreeable. We would take the honeymoon we had missed. So in mid-December we departed Oxford for a Channel port, leaving after supper to catch an overnight ferry. Shortly we encountered the dense, gray-flannel air of a London fog. I drove at ten miles an hour with my left wheels in the barely visible gutter. (Traffic, sensibly, was light.) At every crossroad the gutter disappeared, and Kirby left her seat to walk a foot in front of the Morris, cautiously scanning left and right for headlights. I crept forward behind her. Shakily, we drove the car onto the ferry, slept across the Channel, and descended to France in a dawn without fog. It was comfortable to drive on the right side of the road, as we scooted by stately poplars, past cafés where workers parked bicycles to sip the first cognac of the day.

We entered Germany and spent one night on our way to Vienna. It was only seven years after the war, and the innkeeper was in his thirties, thick-necked and brawny. I could hardly look at him. Vienna was still a four-power city, and we found our hotel in the American sector. The first morning we visited the Soviet embassy for the documents required to exit Austria through the Russian zone to Yugoslavia. We bided our time while the people's bureaucracy bided *its* time. Vienna was restful. I worked on poems. It was the moment of the Orson Welles film, and at every café Kirby and I heard the *Third Man* theme played on a zither.

Kirby had turned twenty-one the month before, and I was

twenty-four. It was the era of early marriages, often brief ones. We had told our parents about our excursion, in letters they would receive only after our departure. We were children trying adulthood out, and we did not want to deal with their worries. After a week of Vienna we received our papers, gassed up, and left the city through the bleak Soviet zone. The bridges were guarded by uniformed teenagers armed with tommy guns. During the drive from Vienna to the Yugoslavian border, I have no memory of stopping to fill up with gas or to eat — which we must have done — until we came to the border and the man directed us to Zagreb.

We drove in the early December darkness into a crowded city and registered with InTourist, a government bureau that required travelers to report their movements. Dinner throughout Yugoslavia was fried indistinguishable meat (maybe mutton) accompanied by fried corn and fried peas. We woke to a cold morning, put on the heavy sweaters Kirby had packed, and set off for Belgrade, traveling from Croatia to Serbia without knowing it. In 1952 the murderous ethnic divisions that would lead to the fracture of the country already existed. We only knew that the nation was arbitrary, created by Versailles largely out of the defunct Austro-Hungarian Empire. In Yugoslavia during the second war, I remembered, two armies of anti-Nazi partisans fought each other as much as they did the Germans, one force led by Mihailović and the other by Tito. After the war, after Yalta, Yugoslavia belonged to Marshal Tito and the Soviet bloc.

The road was two-laned, the landscape dour, as gray as the skies. Belgrade was sophisticated, dense with promenaders, and large enough to confuse a driver. We had no idea where we were, and it was difficult to ask directions because of our defective Serbo-Croatian. (A second language in Yugoslavia was German.) Parked and desperate, I spoke English words and French at random among the walkers. Finally I found a Yugoslav who spoke French as badly as I did — Kirby's was better but she stayed in the car — and we talked in sign language, with an occasional "*tout droit*" or "*à gauche.*" Finally we found InTourist and our hotel, which was comfortable enough, with huge bolsters on the bed. In the morning we checked out of our hotel with a clerk who had English. We told him we were driving to Niš, pronounced Neesh, and his face collapsed. "From Belgrade to Kragujevac there are second-class roads," he told us. "From Kragujevac on" — he paused a foreboding pause — "there are *third-class roads!*"

We drove to Kragujevac over a hilly landscape, icy patches on the road but no snow. We bought more *benzine* and headed toward Niš. Our route became a grassy track winding among obstacles. We struggled through shallow streams. Sometimes we saw nothing like a road ahead, but glimpsed two ruts that emerged from a lumpy valley. Once, as we chugged through a field of mud, our Morris sank to its hubcaps and would not move. Five men working with shovels came to our aid, lifted the car and carried it to firm ground. We remained excited by our adventure — and by being wholly alone for the first time.

We climbed hills, shifting down, then braked as we descended. We caught glimpses across the way of an unfinished sturdy superhighway running parallel to our rutted path. Concrete pylons stood elevated on each side of a river, no bridges yet constructed. We saw in the distance mountains green with fir. One cliff resembled a profile, a chinless Old Man of the Mountain. Mostly we ignored the landscape because our passage consumed us. All day, as we bounced and teetered in the direction of Niš, we drove without encountering a vehicle, not a car nor a truck nor a bus. When we passed through a village, dense with small houses, we were greeted like an army relieving a siege, everyone cheering as we steered carefully through. Kirby and I waved at boys with bicycles who accompanied us until we left town for the wilderness ahead.

We exclaimed at crucial moments of our journey, but otherwise I don't remember that we talked a great deal, and we never quarreled. It was as if we were not yet married. Between our college dating and our wedding, there was a year of separation, with our contact only by mail. Kirby was younger than her years, not in intelligence but in experience. In the fifties it was rare for a girl to be six foot one, and her height separated her from her classmates at Miss Fine's School and at Radcliffe. She was shy, with crushes but without boyfriends. I had the usual girlfriends, but our greatest difference was my single-minded literary obsession. I required a wife who remained passive in the face of my determination.

When we passed through increasing clusters of buildings, InTourist directed us to our hotel in Niška Banja, a spa town of thermal waters surrounded by lavish, empty hotels. A man checked us in at the desk, and the same man served us fried dinner in the empty restaurant, then at breakfast brought mush and coffee before we started out. We headed in the direction of Skopje, a city that approaches Greece and has become Macedonian. A pedestrian stuck out her thumb and turned into a hitchhiker. She talked all the way to her village, friendly and un-intelligible. She wore five skirts — Kirby counted — and while we were driving she extracted a small pouch from somewhere and handed us strange, delicious cookies. Kirby detected chicken fat and honey, and added that she had never before encountered a peasant. We drove through postwar Europe as privileged off-spring of the American Century, 1945–1963, RIP. We did not speculate about how Yugoslavs lived. They might as well have been unfinished concrete highways.

The journey from Niška Banja to Skopje — as on the day be-fore — never revealed another car. There were no gas stations, but someone had given us instructions. Halfway between the villages there was a military dump where we could find gas. I stopped the car, got out, shouted *"Benzine! Benzine!"* and chil-dren pointed to a pitted track. Bicycles led the way. Out of town a mile or so, we came to a fenced-in compound thick with rusty barrels, odds and ends of metal, and one or two collapsed trucks. It did not look military. A middle-aged man opened the gates and motioned us to enter. While Kirby stood and stretched her great height, I unscrewed the cap of the gas tank. The caretaker nodded happily, as if excited to have visitors. He rolled a barrel to the car, fitted a funnel into our gas tank, heaved the barrel up, and poured in *benzine*. I screwed the cap back on and pulled dinars from my pocket. Perhaps the price was seventeen hun-dred dinars; I have no idea. He scratched a figure in the dust on the trunk of the Morris. I handed him, say, two thousand-dinar notes. He shook his head and pointed at the figure. I gestured for him to accept the difference. He thought I didn't get it. He wrote "2000" over "1700," drew a line, and wrote "300." I had no words to tell him that I didn't carry the right change, so I pointed at his inscribed "300" and gestured that it was a tip. He looked agitated, he looked pleased. Kirby and I drove back through the village escorted by bicycles.

At Skopje's InTourist we heard familiar questions. Where had we driven from? I said we came from Belgrade through Niš. The face in front of us looked stricken. "But that is impassable!" he said. An omnibus, he told us, had failed to make the journey two weeks before. "It is impassable!"

"We know," I said, "we know."

When we approached the Greek border we found ourselves driving on an identifiable two-lane road, with bridges across rivers. Friendly, dilatory Greek officers at the border brought us cups of strong coffee as they filled out forms. We talked without language, and proceeded into Greece. The road became lavish with pavement and gas stations. We had arrived at the Marshall Plan. Many houses were painted blue, to signify royalty, since a red army had so recently retreated north into Albania. Walls were still pocked with bullet holes. The day was warm and we took the convertible's top down. Halfway to Salonika we stopped to buy lunch from a street vendor. Sign language provided us a loaf of rugged bread and a wedge of sharp white cheese.

We approached Athens from the north in early twilight, climbing a hill. When we reached its peak we were dazzled to look down and see the Acropolis struck by one beam of the setting sun, as if it posed for its picture. Kirby stood up in our open Morris, tall as an Ionian column, and took a Kodachrome. I felt a poem coming. We drove to our destination, a bed-and-breakfast, from which we set out each morning to perform our pilgrimages. We explored the Parthenon, the surrounding Acropolis, and the agora below. Archaeological pits stood open in winter, and Kirby picked up a loom weight, a small terracotta cone with a hole through the top. We visited Tiryns, Mycenae—and drove to Delphi on a day when there was only one other visitor. We stayed overnight near the oracle's habitat.

In Greece every moment brimmed with ruins and history. Our joy in the ancient world was dogged by one shadow. Maybe this time our route back through Yugoslavia would be truly impassable. Would we take the wrong track and spend Oxford's winter term starving on the margin of a fourth-class road? Then we heard at American Express of an alternative that was amazingly cheap and took only half a day. In Piraeus, Athens's port city, we hoisted the Morris onto a boat and crossed the Adriatic to Brindisi, at the heel of Italy's boot. Early in 1953, we replaced Yugoslavia's one road with Ravenna's mosaics, and continued north through Italy, at first with the convertible's top down. We stopped a few days in Paris, with George Plimpton and other *Paris Review* companions. We crossed the Channel in clear air to Banbury Road.

The marriage lasted fifteen years, ending in 1967. Divorce was miserable, as it always is, and we divorce for the same reasons we marry. I grew up in a comfortable 1920s suburb. Kirby's family raised sugar cane on a plantation in Jamaica. Our tastes in daily life diverged as much as our backgrounds. My literary ambition did not fit with Kirby's reserve. These differences, at first exotic, turned noxious and destructive. Years later I remarried, and in

1975 moved with Jane to my old family farm in New Hampshire. Kirby never remarried. After her own psychoanalysis, she became a psychotherapist, highly regarded in Ann Arbor, where I had taught. She became independent, active, and political. We kept in touch until our two children grew up. Kirby left Michigan in 1991 and settled in the East, to be near our son and daughter, who had come to New England for college and work, and near our grandchildren. Although we lived not far apart, over a dozen years we never saw each other. When a child or a grandchild had a birthday, there were two parties.

Then Kirby became sick, and sicker — misery for children and grandchildren, melancholy and regret for me. Yet to my surprise and gratitude, it brought us together again, and it was a comfort to sit beside her and reminisce. We talked about a journey from Oxford to Athens. But there are no happy endings, because if things are happy they have not ended. Kirby died of cancer in 2008 when she was seventy-six. I survive into my eighties, writing, and oddly cheerful, although disabled and largely alone. There is only one road.

Thank You Thank You

APRIL IS POETRY MONTH, the Academy of American Poets tells us. In 2013 there were 7,427 poetry readings in April, many on a Thursday. For anyone born in 1928 who pays attention to poetry, the numerousness is astonishing. In April of 1948, there were 15 readings in the United States, 12 by Robert Frost.

So I claim. The figures are imaginary, but you get the point.

Whenever a poet comes to the end of a poetry reading, she pauses a moment, then, as a signal for applause, says "Thank you" and nods her head. Hands clap, and she says "Thank you" again, to more applause. Sometimes she says it one more time, or he does. How else does the audience know that the reading might not go on for six hours?

For better or worse, poetry is my life. After a reading, I enjoy the question period. On a tour in Nebraska I read poems to high school kids, a big auditorium. When I finished, someone wanted to know how I got started. I said how at twelve I loved horror movies, then read Edgar Allan Poe, then . . . A young man up front waved his hand. I paused in my story. He asked, "Didn't you do it to pick up chicks?"

I remembered cheerleaders at Hamden High School. "It works better," I told him, "when you get older."

It used to be that one poet in each generation performed poems in public. In the twenties it was Vachel Lindsay, who sometimes dropped to his knees in the middle of a poem. Then Robert Frost took over, and made his living largely on the road. He spoke well, his meter accommodating his natural sentences, and in between poems he made people laugh. At times onstage he played the chicken farmer, cute and countrified, eliciting coos of delight from an adoring audience. Once, after I heard him do this routine, I attended the post-reading cocktail party, where he ate deviled eggs, sipped martinis, and slaughtered the reputations of Eliot, Williams, Stevens, Moore . . .

Back then, other famous poets read aloud only two or three times a year. If they were alive now, probably they could make a better living saying their poems than they did as an editor at Faber and Faber, or an obstetrician, or an insurance company executive, or a Brooklyn librarian.

In 1952 I recited aloud the first time, booming in Oxford's Sheldonian Theatre from a bad poem that had won a prize. The London *Times* remarked on my "appropriately lugubrious voice." When I first did a full-length poetry reading, three years later, my arms plunged stiff from my shoulders, my voice was changeless in pitch and volume, my face rigid, expressionless, pale — as if I were a collaborator facing a firing squad.

A question period for undergraduates at a Florida college began with the usual stuff: what is the difference between poetry and prose? Then I heard a question I had never heard before: "How do you reconcile being a poet with being president of Hallmark cards?" This inquisitive student had looked on the Internet and learned that the man who runs the sentiment factory is indeed Donald Hall.

It's a common name. Once before a reading a man asked me, "Are you Donald Hall?"

"Yes," I said.

"So am I," he said.

At the end of the airport's titanium tube a man carried a sign with the poet's name. The assistant professor drove her an hour to his campus, talking nervously all the way about whether he'd get tenure from his English department. When he drove her back for her flight the next day, he asked her to write a letter of recommendation.

When my first book came out in 1955, it was praised, I did a second book, my poems appeared in magazines — but nobody asked me to speak them out loud. I taught at the University of Michigan, which sponsored no readings. To my students I recited great poems with gusto and growing confidence — Wyatt, Keats, Dickinson, Whitman, Yeats, Hardy — and worked on performance without knowing it. It was a shock when a lecture agent telephoned to offer a fee for reading my poems at a college. It happened again, and I flew off on days when I didn't teach. Michigan paid minimal salaries, and most teachers amplified their incomes by plodding to summer school. I stayed home and wrote instead of employing the Socratic method in a suffocating classroom.

As the phone kept ringing, I supposed that poetry readings were some sort of fad, like cramming into phone booths; I would enjoy it as long as it lasted.

When my generation learned to read aloud, publishing from platforms more often than in print, we heard our poems change. Sound had always been my portal to poetry, but in the beginning sound was imagined through the eye. Gradually the out-loud mouth-juice of vowels, or mouth-chunk of consonants, gave body to poems in performance. Dylan Thomas showed the way. Charles Olson said that "form is never more than an extension of content." Really, content is only an excuse for oral sex. The most erotic poem in English is *Paradise Lost*.

In concentrating on sound, as in anything else, there are things to beware of. Revising a poem one morning, I found myself knowing that a new phrase was a cliché or a dead metaphor, but realizing that I could intone it aloud so that it would pass. Watch out. A poem must work from the platform but it must also work on the page. My generation started when poetry was print, before it became sound. We were lucky to practice both modes at once.

· · ·

A chairman of English warned a friend of mine about her approaching audience. "They're *required* to attend," he said. "They don't listen to *anything*. Sometimes in class I ask them to open a window, or to close it, just to see if they're *alive*." He sighed a deep sigh, as ponderous as tenure. "I don't know what I'd *do* if the *New Yorker* didn't come on Thursdays."

It's alleged that Homer said his poems aloud. Somewhat later, we hear that Tennyson read his poems to Queen Victoria, but we don't hear much more. In the 1930s William Butler Yeats traveled by train across America, from East Coast to West, but the master of mellifluous stanzas didn't speak his verses. At universities, to butter his bread, he read the typescript of a lecture called "Three Great Irishmen." Maybe poets used to be paid *not* to say their poems?

By chance, I had been an undergraduate at the one college in America with an endowed series of poetry readings. Eliot was good, but most performances were insufferable — superb poems spoken as if they were lines from the telephone book. William Carlos Williams read too quickly in a high-pitched voice, but seemed to enjoy himself. Wallace Stevens appeared to loathe his beautiful work, making it flat and half audible. (Maybe he thought the boys in the office would tease him.) Marianne Moore's tuneless drone was as eccentric as her inimitable art. When she spoke between poems, Moore mumbled in an identical monotone. Since she frequently revised or cut her things, a listener had to concentrate, to distinguish poems from talk. After twenty minutes she looked distressed, and said "Thank you." When Dylan Thomas read, I hovered above the auditorium seat as I heard him say Yeats's "Lapis Lazuli." He read his own poems afterward, fabricated for his rich and succulent Welsh organ. I found myself floating again. In four American visits, from 1950 to 1953, when he died in New York, Thomas read his poems many times at many places, from New York's Poetry Center through dozens of western colleges. Frost's eminence among poetry readers disappeared for a time.

In a question period I launched into my familiar rant about dead metaphors, asserting that when "I am glued to the chair" equals "I am anchored to the spot," we claim that a tugboat is Elmer's Glue. This afternoon I was obsessed with clichés using disability metaphors: the *crippled* economy, *blind* ambition, *deaf* to entreaties, the *paralysis* of industry, and . . .

At the end I summed up my argument. Guileless, I said, "All these metaphors are lame."

Why was everyone laughing?

Dylan Thomas's popularity was not only on account of his voice or his verse. Thomas was a *star,* and most people came to his readings because of the Tales of Master Dylan — vast drunkenness, creative obscenity at parties, botched seductions, nightly comas — but if people attended because of his celebrity, at least they were going to a poetry reading. Maybe the explosion of recitation was also because of a cultural change. Songs were no longer Tin Pan Alley, and the lyrics were worth heeding. When everyone listened to Bob Dylan, they heard lines that resembled poetry. When people *heard* memorable language sung from platforms, they became able to *hear* poems recited in auditoriums. The University of Michigan began to schedule poetry readings every Tuesday at four p.m. A gathering of students, sometimes three hundred, attended each week and absorbed what they listened to. A few days after one reading I met Sarah, a friend of my daughter's. She recited a stanza from Tuesday's poet. "You've been reading her books!" I said. Oh, no, she said. Sarah *remembered* what the poet recited.

Once after a circuit reading, my driver left me at a house for a party. I would spend the night there, while he went to a motel to get some sleep, and he would pick me up the next morning at six. The party was good; the party was long. These were the days when people drank liquor. Our host drooped asleep on the sofa at four a.m., which was apparently his daily wont. I didn't notice because I was flirting with a pretty woman, whose husband stood dazed beside her, until he emerged into consciousness to attack me. His fist aimed at my jaw but moved so slowly that I was able to duck. Three minutes later, we became friends forever, and at six a.m. I stood on the sidewalk waiting for my escort to drive me to the next reading, the next party.

After a poet friend performed in Mississippi one winter, a man handed her a heavy box of typewriter paper, saying, "I want to share my poems with you." When she glanced through "Verses of a Sergeant Major, Ret.," she found it unreadable. Telling me about it, she asserted that "share" has become a verb of assault disguised as magnanimity. "Unless you read my poems, I will gouge your eyeballs out."

Bert Hornback ran the Tuesday readings in Ann Arbor, supplementing the English department's pittance by appealing to university administrators for discretionary funds. After ten years of weekly readings he burned out, and watched as the feckless department dropped to holding one reading a year. He decided to see what he could do by himself. On a January day in the eighties he rented the university's Rackham Auditorium, sold tickets for a joint poetry reading — $5.50 each, 50 cents to Ticketmaster — and invited some friends to read: Wendell Berry, Galway Kinnell, Sharon Olds, and Seamus Heaney — long before Seamus went to Stockholm. On a Friday night — against a home basketball game, against the Chicago Symphony — Bert filled eleven hundred seats with paying poetry fans. The fire department permitted a hundred standing-room-only tickets, which sold out, and Bert added further SROs when the fire department wasn't looking. Unexpected vanloads arrived from Cleveland, Chicago, Milwaukee, and Michigan's Upper Peninsula. Each poet read for forty minutes, and after a break did ten minutes more. Outside, the crowd without tickets sulked and grumbled. It was said that scalpers charged as much as $50.

A Dodge Festival in New Jersey was massive with poets, schoolteachers, and schoolkids. Each poet did panels, question periods, and readings. The first night all twenty-five poets read, a few minutes each, to a crowd of three thousand. Nobody sitting at the back of the tent could have seen a poet's face if the festival had not enlarged each visage on a screen like the Dallas Cowboys'. For close-ups the Dodge employed a black-jointed steel arm, a foot thick and fifty feet long, which curled and lurched its camera back and forth, grabbing each facial detail in its metallic tentacles. It looked as if it were searching for a source of protein.

A week after the readings and lectures of the festival, last year's Pulitzer poet received a thick letter from a woman in South Carolina who had fallen in love. The envelope was heavy with amorous poems, and she told him that there were ninety-seven more, but she didn't have the stamps. She attached a photograph of a mature woman in front of a ranch house, and implored him to fly down immediately. She enclosed an airline ticket with blank dates.

It's okay to be pleased when an audience loves you, or treats you as deathless, but you must not believe it. Someone says that my reading is the best she has ever heard; a man tells me that he has read me for thirty years and that I am a giant in American letters. I know I'm not. Doubtless many praisers believe such extravagance when they say it, and it does no good to argue. I could tell them nasty things people have said about me in print. I could list the prizes I have not won and the anthologies from which I have been omitted. It is best to believe the praiser and dismiss the praise. Nine-tenths of the contemporary poets who win prizes and praises, who are applauded the most, who are treated everywhere like emperors — or like statues of emperors — will go unread in thirty years. If a poet is any good, how would the listeners *know?* Poets have no notion of their own durability or distinction. When poets announce that their poems are immortal, they are depressed or lying or psychotic. Interviewing T. S. Eliot, I saved my cheekiest question for last. "Do you know you're any good?" His revised and printed response was formal, but in person he was abrupt: "Heavens no! Do you? Nobody intelligent knows if he's any good."

Look at the sad parade of Poets Laureate.

Sometimes an audience is not three thousand. A friend of mine arrived at a hall to find that his listener was singular. They went out for a beer. I heard of another poet who showed up for a crowd of two. Gamely, she did a full reading from the podium, and afterward descended to shake the hands of her crowd. One was dead.

When I was young I could project, and now without a microphone I can't be heard in the tenth row. It's not only the debility of age. One's range is diminished by habitual use of microphones. (When stage actors spend twenty years making movies, they are inaudible when they return to Broadway or the West End.) But there are advantages to artificial enhancement. There's a poem in which I moo like a cow. Cows' lungs are bigger than ours. I approach the microphone intimately, and softly but audibly moo as long as a cow moos. Proximity to the microphone saves my wind as I croon, *"Mm-mmm-mmmmm-mmmmmmmm-uggh wanchhh."* My friends say it's the best line I've ever written.

After the group-talk of the question period comes the poet-and-one. People line up for signatures. Sometimes the seeker dictates a dedication, "Say, 'With love to Billy and his adorable wife Sheila who makes a great pound cake.'" The signer should demur, or at least edit. Everyone in line must spell a name, or "Felicia" turns out to be "Phylysha." (Once at a prep school a boy asked me to write, "For Mom and Dad." I said that my parents were dead. We worked things out.) If there are just a few in line, the poet can speak with them as if they were people. If the line is long, it becomes impossible to distinguish one petitioner from another. At the end stands the host — the man who invited the poet to the campus, who picked her up at the airport, with whom she had a lengthy conversation, who will give her the check, who hands her a book to sign — and she has no idea of his name.

Once I read at a college in Minnesota. As the dean led me up the platform, he told me something he had forgotten: I should read for only twenty-five minutes, instead of the contracted fifty, because after my presentation the students would elect this year's Homecoming Queen. The auditorium was packed. (At lunch afterward, English professors told me that they had entered the auditorium astonished: so many students for a poetry reading!) After I read, the applause was long. An audience applauds longest when it knows it has not been paying attention. A young woman wearing a ball gown and a gold crown ascended the platform and stood at the rostrum where I had stood. She was last year's Homecoming Queen, who would preside over this year's vote and coronation. Six girls in ball gowns hovered in the wings. "*Now*," said the retiring Queen, "*now* comes the moment you've all been waiting for!"

The dean sitting beside me on the platform whispered in my ear, "She doesn't mean it the way it sounds!"

• • •

Once I flew half a day to be picked up in Oklahoma for a reading the next morning in a corner of Arkansas, to read at chapel — a compulsory gathering of all students — at a small Christian college. Sometimes at such places a self-satisfied piety hovers over faculty and students like smog in Los Angeles. Sometimes these places are lively and responsive. It's hard to plan what to read, but I would never choose a poem to *épater* my hosts. This time, three people picked me up — a woman who chaired English, shy, who spoke little; a man who ran Humanities, thrilled by poetry and ample in literary knowledge; and the older woman who had brought me there, I think a dean of Honors, who was ebullient and talkative, funny and smart and warm. Because we had a long way to drive, we stopped outside the airport for supper before continuing. I was returning from the men's room when I heard the dean address her companions: "Well, Ah'm going to *tell* him."

As I sat, she turned to me and spoke sweetly — smiling broadly, saying what she needed to say, unashamed of her language: "Donald, if you say 'fuck' in chapel tomorrow, Ah'll get *fahrd.*"

Some readings prove memorable for a single eccentricity. On an occasion in Lancaster, Pennsylvania, an orchestra was finishing rehearsal in the auditorium as the poetry reading was due to begin. Introducer and poet carried music stands into the wings. In London a reading was to begin at six p.m. in the ancient Church of St. Giles-in-the-Fields. Evensong prevailed. Another time, in the state of Chiapas in Mexico, eight writers sat onstage waiting hours for the governor to arrive. A large audience had departed by the time he walked in, surrounded by bodyguards with machine guns. In fatigue we each read to the governor for five minutes.

"*Gracias,*" we said. "*Gracias.*"

As I limped into my eighties, my readings altered, as everything did. Performance held up, but not body; I had to read sitting down. When an introduction slogged to its end, I lurched from backstage, hobbled, and carefully aimed my ass into a chair. For a while I began each reading with a short poem I was trying out, which spoke of being eleven and watching my grandfather milk his Holsteins. In the poem I asked, in effect, how my grandfather would respond if he saw me now. When I finished saying the poem, there was always a grave pause, long enough to drive a hayrack through, followed by a standing ovation. Earlier, I had never received a standing O after a first poem; now it happened again and again, from Pennsylvania to Minnesota to California, and I thought I had written something uncannily moving. When I mailed copies of the poem to friends for praise, they politely told me it was terrible. I was puzzled and distressed, until I figured it out. The audience had just seen me stagger, waver with a cane, and labor to sit down, wheezing. They imagined my grandfather horrified, watching a cadaver gifted with speech. They stood and applauded because they knew they would never see me again.

Three Beards

IN MY LIFE I have grown three beards, covering many of my adult faces. My present hairiness is monumental, and I intend to carry it into the grave. (I must avoid chemotherapy.) A woman has instigated each beard, the original bush requested by my first wife Kirby. Why did she want it? Maybe she was tired of the same old face. Or maybe she thought a beard would be raffish; I did. In the fifties, no one wore beards. In Eisenhower's day, as in the time of the Founding Fathers, all chins were smooth, and during the Civil War beards were as common as sepsis. Both my New Hampshire great-grandfathers wore facial hair, the Copperhead who fought in the war and the sheep farmer too old for combat. By the time I was sentient, in the 1930s, only my eccentric cousin Freeman was bearded, and even he shaved once in summer. Every September he endured a fortnight of scratchiness. Many men, after trying a beard for five or six days, want to claw off their skin. They pick up their Gillettes.

Despite the itch, I persisted until I looked something like a Mathew Brady photograph, or at least not like a professor of

English literature at the University of Michigan. The elderly chairman of the department was intelligent and crafty. When he spoke in well-constructed paragraphs, with inviolate syntax, he sounded like a member of Parliament — except for his midwestern accent. He always addressed me as "Hall," and used last names for all his staff. The summer of the beard I dropped in at the department to pick up my mail. I wore plastic flip-flops, sagging striped shorts, a Detroit Tigers T-shirt, and a grubby stubble like today's male models in *Vanity Fair.* My chairman greeted me, noting my rank: "Good morning, Professor Hall."

Dinner parties and cocktail parties dominated every Ann Arbor weekend. Women wore girdles; the jacket pockets of men's gray suits showed the fangs of handkerchiefs. Among the smooth-faced crowds of Chesterfield smokers, I enjoyed cigars, which added to the singularity of my beard and rendered living rooms uninhabitable. When I lectured to students I walked up and down with my cigar, dropping ashes in a tin wastebasket. The girls in the front row smoked cigarettes pulled from soft blue leather pouches stamped with golden fleurs-de-lis. As the sixties began, if I was sluggish beginning my lecture — maybe I had stayed up all night with a visiting poet — I paused by the front row and asked if anyone had some of those diet things. Immediately, female hands held forth little ceramic boxes full of spansules or round pink pills. After I ingested Dexedrine, my lecture speeded up and rose in pitch until only dogs could hear it.

When I was bearded and my mother visited me, she stared at the floor, addressing me without making eye contact. Why did she hate beards so intensely? She adored her hairy grandfathers

and her cousin Freeman. Her father Wesley, of the next generation, shaved once or twice a week. On Saturday night before
Sunday's church, Wesley perched on a set tub. Looking into the
mirror of a twenty-five-hour clock, he scraped his chin with a
straight razor.

In 1967 my marriage, which had faltered for years, splintered and
fell apart. As Vietnam conquered American campuses, I hung
out with students who weaned me from cigars to cigar joints.
"Make love not war" brought chicks and dudes together, rais-
ing everyone's political consciousness. Middle-class boys from
Bloomfield Hills proved they belonged to the Movement by beg-
ging on the streets for spare change.

I signed the last divorce papers while anesthetized for a biopsy
of my left testicle. The tumor was benign, but divorces aren't.
I shaved because the world had altered. Although my mother
fretted about the divorce, she looked at my face again. My sud-
den singleness and my naked skin confused my friends. I was
still invited to dinner parties, and therefore gave dinner parties
back. I invited eight people for dinner. When I noticed that I had
no placemats, I substituted used but laundered diapers, which I
had bought for drying dishes. For dinner I served two entrées,
Turkey Salad Amaryllis and Miracle Beans. I bought three turkey rolls, cooked them and chopped them up with onions and
celery, then added basil and two jars of Hellmann's Real. It was
delicious, and so were Miracle Beans. Warm ten cans of B&Ms,
add garlic, add basil again, add dry mustard, stir, and serve.

My friends enjoyed my dinner parties. I served eight bottles of chilled Chassagne-Montrachet Cailleret, Louis Latour.

Five years later I married Jane, then a poetry student, who by the time of her death in 1995 had published four books and earned a Guggenheim. It was exhilarating to live with her as her work became better and better. The more successful her poetry became, the more she permitted herself to be pretty. Late photographs of Jane reveal two sides, both beautiful. In one she is utterly spiritual, almost ready to turn bodiless; in another she is horny. Her poetry combined the two Janes, which is exactly what poems must do. When we married I was clean-shaven. She looked at old photographs and decided that I should grow a beard again. She observed my itchy agony. She wrote a poem called "The First Eight Days of the Beard."

> 1. *A page of exclamation points.*
> 2. *A class of cadets at attention.*
> 3. *A school of eels.*
> 4. *Standing commuters.*
> 5. *A bed of nails for the swami.*
> 6. *Flagpoles of unknown countries.*
> 7. *Centipedes resting on their laurels.*
> 8. *The toenails of the face.*

After a few weeks my facial hair looked like a beard, not like carelessness, and after two months it flourished. I wished it would hang straight down and cover my belly, but it always grew tightly curled, as pubic as Santa Claus.

For three years we stayed in Ann Arbor. We loved the house we lived in, old-fashioned with many bedrooms, but it rose in a crowded part of town, and we did not like living among people. Once a year we visited the farmhouse in New Hampshire, where my grandmother Kate survived in her nineties, and where I had spent childhood summers. We could see from the porch a cottage down the road, built for a farmhand in the 1890s, and nothing else that resembled a house. Jane fell in love with this 1803 solitary clapboard structure with its 1865 barn and collapsing sugarhouse. It backed up to Ragged Mountain, which had provided pasturage for my grandfather's cattle. Mount Kearsarge was five miles south. Fields of grass filled the narrow valleys. She loved Thornley's Store down the street — wine and stovepipe, roast beef and souvenir ashtrays — where in the morning the neighborhood gathered to joke and gossip. We drove gawking on dirt roads around Eagle Pond, through a pig farm, and up New Canada Road past Freeman's collapsed shack. During one visit on a Sunday we attended the South Danbury Christian Church, where my grandmother played the organ for eighty years. My cousins called me "Donnie" and the preacher quoted "Rilke the German poet."

After my grandmother entered the Peabody Home, we agreed with my mother and her sisters that we would buy the farmhouse when my grandmother died. In 1975 I quit my tenure and we moved to New Hampshire. It was daunting to pay for groceries and the mortgage by freelance writing — but it worked and I loved doing it. Our move made for the best years of our existence. My poems improved, and I wrote magazine pieces about baseball and New Hampshire. Year after year Jane committed to the life of poetry and we thrived in double solitude. (The New Hampshire Constitution prohibits dinner parties.) One day followed another, a bliss of sameness — and I plotted a distraction.

After sporting my beard for thirteen years, I would shave it off in secret on Christmas Day. I bought a can of Barbasol shaving cream and a packet of disposable razors, which I hid in the bathroom with a sharp pair of scissors. That Christmas we had a houseful. My mother Lucy came, Jane's mother Polly, and my college-age children Andrew and Philippa. Christmas morning we had breakfast followed by the opening of presents. Then came the sleepy interlude while the turkey cooked. I waited until it seemed that everyone had used the bathroom. I sneaked in, closed the door, and unpacked my tools. I picked up the shears and looked at my face in the mirror over the sink. I hesitated. Did I really want to do this? My qualms disappeared when I thought of the family dozing in the living room. With scissors I cut great clumps of hair from my chin and cheeks, depositing handfuls in the wastebasket. Careful not to dig a hole in my face, I removed the bulk of my hair. The tufts left behind were like a hayfield ill cut, ragged clumps sprouting here and there. I lathered and applied the razor. Every inch I scraped, the razor filled up and clogged. I cleaned it under the faucet. My flesh appeared as it had before "The First Eight Days of the Beard" — with a new sag of chin.

Into the living room I walked. Philippa screamed. Jane and her mother ran from the kitchen horrified, ready to dial 911. Hubbub rattled the plaster on the walls. My mother stared with her mouth open, then grinned. Only Andrew smiled calmly, enjoying my trick on the family world. Through turkey and stuffing, I was aware of eyes that kept looking up to confirm the new face. After three pies on a warm Christmas afternoon, Andrew sat me down on the porch and trimmed away the remaining fuzz. In the days following, responses from the local world were mostly bewilderment, followed by laughter. The farrier who had repaired the range, however, refused to believe it was me. I was pulling out my license, in the store down the street, before Bob Thornley convinced him. My uncle Dick, on the other hand, didn't notice the alteration. He thought I looked different but wasn't sure why.

My face remained naked as long as Jane was alive. We were photographed together, and Bill Moyers did a show called *A Life Together*. Occasionally today the film is shown in my presence, and I need to proclaim that I am not an imposter.

Jane died at forty-seven after fifteen months of leukemia. I mourned her deeply, I wrote nothing but elegy, I wailed her loss, but — as I excused myself in a poem — "Lust is grief / that has turned over in bed / to look the other way." Among spousal survivors, many cannot bear the thought of another lover. Some cannot do without. In *Ulysses,* Leopold Bloom thinks of a graveyard as a place to pick up a grieving widow. Thus I found myself in the pleasant company of a young woman who worked for a magazine — a slim, pretty blonde who was funny, sharp, and promiscuous. (We never spoke of *love.*) I will call her Pearl. After dinner, we sat in my living room drinking Madeira and talking. I pulled out a cigarette and asked her if she would mind . . . "I was going crazy," she said, and pulled out her own. She told me about her father's suicide. I spoke of Jane's death. When she left the room to pee, I waited by the bathroom door for her to emerge. I led her unprotesting to the bedroom, and a few moments later, gaily engaged, she said, "I want to put my legs around your head." (It was perfect iambic pentameter.) When we woke in the morning we became friends. We drank coffee and smoked. When I spoke again of Jane, Pearl said that perhaps I felt a bit happier this morning.

After seven weeks Pearl ended things. Before I received my dismissal, we lay in the backyard sunning, and she suggested I grow a beard. She had seen book jackets. "You'll look Mephistophelian," she said. That's all I needed. It suited me again to change the way I looked because the world had utterly changed. I mourned Jane all day every day, and acknowledged her death by the third beard and the girlfriends. Some entanglements ended because I was needy, others because of adultery or my gradual physical disability. A California friend and I commuted to visit each other for more than a year. She diminished my beard by trimming it into a goatee, getting me to smooth my cheeks from sideburns to mustache and chin. After dozens of assignations amassing airline mileage, we decided we had had enough. I grew the big beard back.

A dozen years ago I found Linda and love again. We live an hour apart but spend two or three nights a week together. She is an Old Lady of the Mountain in her bone structure, with pretty dimples. She is tender and as sloppy as I am. She abjures earrings, makeup, and dresses; she wears blue jeans and yard-sale shirts. Combs and brushes are for sissies. We watch movies, we read Edith Wharton to each other, and we travel. In 2002 we impulsively flew to London, and later we took many trips for poetry readings without ever combing our hair.

When I turned eighty and rubbed testosterone onto my chest, my beard roared like a lion and lengthened four inches. The hair on my head grew longer and more jumbled, and with Linda's encouragement I never restrained its fury. As Linda wheelchaired me through airports, and my eighties prolonged, more than ever I enjoyed being grubby and noticeable. Declining more swiftly toward the grave, I make certain that everyone knows — my children know, Linda knows, my undertaker knows — that no posthumous razor may scrape my blue face.

No Smoking

WHEN I LOOK at the barn in my ninth decade, I see the NO SMOKING sign, rusted and tilting on the unpainted gray clapboard. My grandfather, born in 1875, milked his cattle there a century ago. None of my grandparents smoked. I don't know when my grandfather nailed up the sign, but I know why. Sometimes a tramp would dodge inside the barn after dark to sleep on a bed of hay, and once my grandfather found cigarette ash when he climbed to the tie-up in the morning. It doesn't take much to burn down a barn. Whenever I focus on the sign, white letters against red, I pull a cigarette from the pack beside me, flick my Bic, and take a drag.

When my parents and I visited the farm, way back, my father was required to do his smoking outside. My mother, who learned to smoke when she went to college, pretended to her parents that she never touched the stuff. (My grandmother lived to be ninety-seven, and her sense of smell diminished. My elderly mother sneaked upstairs and puffed on a cigarette.) My father was a gentle and supportive man, but he was tense, shaky — and could not do without his Chesterfields. He walked up and down the driveway, dodging horse manure, to work on his four-pack-a-day habit. He started smoking when he was fourteen and wasn't diagnosed with lung cancer until 1955, when he was fifty-one. Every time I write, say, or think "lung cancer," I pick up a Pall Mall to calm myself.

In 1955 I lived with my wife and baby son about two hours away from my parents. In May I drove down for my father's exploratory operation, and pushed his gurney into the elevator. My mother and I drove home to wait for the telephone call. If the phone did not ring for half a day, it could mean that the cancerous lung had been removed. The telephone rang too soon. When we arrived at the surgeon's office, Dr. Appel told us that he could not extract the tumor without killing my father. He said the short-term prospects were fine, but the long-term . . . (My father's radiation would give him two good months. He played golf, and didn't die until December.) As my mother realized what Dr. Appel was telling us, her fingers twitched at her purse. For her convenience, the thoracic surgeon pushed his ashtray to the edge of the desk.

Everyone smoked in 1955. When adults had a party, they set out cigarettes in leather boxes on every table, every mantelpiece, every flat surface, beside silver Ronson lighters among myriad ashtrays. There were round crystal ashtrays, and square ones with deep receptacles over ceramic bottoms; there were ashtrays that sprouted from the floor on black steel stems; there were ashtrays with cork humps in the middle, for knocking cinders out of a pipe. In Durham, North Carolina, there is the Duke Homestead and Tobacco Museum. I imagine multiple busy artifacts overcrowding its showcases. There are museums elsewhere, but it would be tedious to visit them all. In Shanghai there's the China Tobacco Museum with Cigarette Exhibition, and there's another in Indonesia.

In her attic, my friend Carole Colburn found a large, impressive volume. The American Tobacco Company published *"Sold American!" The First Fifty Years* to celebrate its birthday, 1904–1954. In 144 pages, nine inches by twelve and bound in bright red, the industry illustrates its development from the sixteenth century, when explorers and colonists first enjoyed the leaf, proffered by generous Indians. There are many companies that were founded to cure tobacco, and there were three means of induction. You could sniff it or chew it or burn it. Fire required devices like pipes, or tobacco wrapped in tobacco, or tobacco rolled inside an alien substance. Paper won out, and in 1904 ten companies combined into the American Tobacco Company.

A foreword by the company's president, Paul M. Hahn, gives us history. Sir Walter Raleigh helped to spread the addiction to tobacco. George Washington sought it for his troops. We hear of King James I as "the first great tobacco-hater"—a surgeon general of the sixteenth century. Despite the book's many anecdotes, Mr. Hahn never mentions that firing squads pulled their triggers when victims threw away their last cigarettes. He doesn't tell us that Christopher Marlowe, murdered in 1593, died declaring, "All they that love not Tobacco and Boys are fools!"

We hear of cigar store Indians. We hear of Sweet Caporal, LS/MFT (Lucky Strike Means Fine Tobacco), Herbert Tareyton . . .

We see woodcuts of farmers growing tobacco, commissioned by the American Tobacco Company and executed by Thomas Hart Benton. We hear how Franklin Delano Roosevelt switched from cigars to cigarettes, which he sported in a fashionable long holder. It was during the Great War that cigarettes conquered both sides of the trenches. From the Revolution through the Civil War to the Second World War, tobacco enhanced and facilitated slaughter.

Nowhere can I find the American Tobacco Company's centennial sequel: *"Harmful to Your Health!" The First Hundred Years.* I tried Amazon.

For fifty years, all American living rooms turned dense with smoke, as did bars, restaurants, hardware stores, hotel lobbies, cabins, business offices, factory floors, sedans, hospital rooms, pizzerias, sweatshops, town meetings, laboratories, palaces, department stores, supermarkets, barbershops, McDonald's, beauty parlors, art galleries, bookstores, pharmacies, men's rooms, corner groceries, women's rooms, barns except for my grandfather's, movie houses, dairies, airports, offices of thoracic surgeons, depots, tearooms, Automats, cafeterias, town halls, Macy's, gymnasiums, igloos, waiting rooms, museums, newsrooms, classrooms, steel mills, libraries, lecture halls, emergency rooms, auditoriums, parks, Mongolian yurts, and beaches — not to mention funeral parlors.

Tidying up living rooms after parties, host and hostess filled garbage cans with a thousand cigarette butts. Ashes and ground-out cigarettes outweighed burned toast, eggshells, paper towels, tin cans, hypodermic needles, and kitty litter. In 1954 twenty-three cents bought a pack of cigarettes. (Now it takes maybe six to nine dollars, even more depending on state taxes.) Hotels didn't need to designate smoking rooms, because people smoked in all the rooms. The back page of every magazine — *Time,* the *Atlantic Monthly, Newsweek, Life* — carried a full-color ad for cigarettes. Retiring boomers remember the Marlboro Man, who suggested that cigarettes enlarged one's penis. Virginia Slims deepened one's cleavage. A prominent advertising theme was medical. A solemn man looked us straight in the eye and pointed his finger at us, the way Uncle Sam recruited us during the Great War. The man wore a white coat with a head mirror and — in case you didn't recognize his profession — a stethoscope draped around his neck. "Old Gold," he told us firmly, "is good for you!"

Then the surgeon general put terrifying labels on each pack, and by the millennium everyone decent knew that smoking was unforgivable, like mass murder or Rush Limbaugh. My dear friend Alice Mattison twice bopped me on the face to dislodge a Kent. At first there were smoking areas in bars and restaurants, but shortly all smoking was forbidden in all public places. Guilty, grubby men and women gathered on sidewalks in front of buildings. Despite blizzards or record heat, people in johnnies stood outside hospitals, a cigarette in one hand and an IV pole in the other. Everyone huddled in shame, bending heads to conceal identity, and took deep drags of emphysema, congestive heart, high blood pressure, heart disease, COPD whatever that is, and cancers of the mouth, esophagus, and lung.

For a moment I interrupt myself. Ah, that's better.

• • •

My friend Carole smokes cigarettes, the only friend who does. When she visits we sit opposite each other, smoking and talking about death. We speak of how, when we're driving or watching a game on TV or reading, we pick up a cigarette, light it, and inhale — in order to have *something to do*. Is it a masturbation substitution? There's one advantage to smoking, about which we agree. When our breathing starts to vanish, we will not ask, "Why me?"

Sentient, sensible human beings flee into the bushes when we exhale. When Linda stays with me, I step outside on the porch to smoke. (From cars passing at night I feel the horror and rage of motorists who witness the red tip of my culpability.) It puts off for a moment the agony of deprived addiction. Depraved. Something I haven't mentioned about the benefit of cigarettes. When I am twisted by a hacking cough — which interrupts me as I read obituaries, or Ira Byock on palliative care — guess what I do to stop the coughing?

Linda praises, with reluctance, another result of my smoking. She accompanies me on poetry readings, and says that my ravaged throat keeps my voice low and resonant. At the end of a reading, people line up for signatures; sometimes, interrupting the customers, I pretend to use the men's room. When I was offered the Poet Laureateship I decided I must turn it down because I couldn't smoke in the Laureate's office; I changed my mind when I learned I could avoid the office. When I visited it, just once in my tenure, a librarian unscrewed a long window that opened onto a secure balcony. At an AWP convention — a writers' group — eight thousand people registered at a Chicago hotel.

When I walked through the lobby to lumber outside and smoke, I was assailed by four hundred emerging poets, and fled as soon as I could. If you smoked in your hotel room, the fine was seven hundred dollars. I cracked the window and smoked in the hotel room. The chambermaid did not snitch.

Kendel Currier is my assistant, who types my drafts and my letters, who bookkeeps, who solves my technical problems, who explains legal and financial documents, and who drives me places. Once she found a cigarette butt in the leather case that I leave for her on my porch. A misplaced cigarette had torched my revisions. "I couldn't find it. I figured it went out." Once when the snow melted, she harvested a bushel basket of soggy butts from the garden by the porch, which I had hurled all winter into snowdrifts. Another time, she drove me in my car all the way to New York, and I courteously opened the window to smoke. Somewhere around Springfield, Massachusetts, she told me I could not smoke in my own car. She parked and I walked up and down a gutter, inhaling relief. Kendel is kind, but Kendel is a hard case.

I came late to cigarettes. When I was young, I smoked cigars in Exeter's butt rooms. (All prep schools provided smoking retreats in each dormitory.) Later I smoked cigars in lecture halls when I taught, and on all social occasions. One friend told me that whenever I smoked coronas at her cocktail parties she sent her drapes to the cleaners. Of course I didn't inhale — I didn't know how — but when I blew out a lungful of cigar smoke, I choked on the murk around me. Everybody did. I even smoked cigars during psychotherapy. Dr. Frolich was a psychoanalyst, the only one in Ann Arbor who did therapy. (There were seven analysts in the city, seven more than in Vienna.) Therapy instead of analysis kept the two of us face-to-face — I didn't lie on a couch — and we met only three times a week, for only four years. While I sat with a smoldering Judges Cave, Dr. Frolich smoked Camels, sometimes lighting a new one from the butt of the old. He had smoked from early adulthood through four years of medical school, while a medic in World War II, during an internship, two years of psychiatric residency, analytic training for five years at an institute, and decades of practice. He was seventy and told me that he finished three cartons a week. During a session late in our progress I noticed that he was not smoking, and remembered that he had not smoked for days. I asked him why, and he told me that his elder son had asked him to stop. Dr. Frolich answered that it would not help him after all these years. When his son replied that he was thinking of secondary smoke and himself, Dr. Frolich stopped smoking. He told me it was easy. He lived to be ninety-two.

Like all smokers I quit from time to time. Once in my sixties I stopped for good, as it seemed. Someone told me about a hypnotist in Concord who cured smokers. I've always been easy to hypnotize; if you have an overdeveloped ego, you are not scared of surrender. The moment I met the doctor, I knew he was a fraud. With a starched white coat, he was as handsome and suave as the model who recommended Old Golds for your health. (I expected him to offer me shares in his Bernie Madoff investment firm, annual dividends guaranteed at ninety percent.) But what the hell? I decided to go ahead and try. In a small room he spoke to me soothingly, his tone impersonating a hypnotist's. When I felt sleepy he turned on a tape of his own voice and left the room.

When the recording finished, I knew I would never smoke again. I left his office feeling ecstatic. Illicitly, I threw a pack in the gutter. For seven weeks I continued to feel blissful without nicotine. Then one night at suppertime, before I would fly to Arkansas in the morning, the phone rang. My dearest friend from school and college, best man at my first wedding, had dropped dead at the age of fifty. Driving to Logan Airport on my way to the reading, I stopped at the first open shop and bought cigarettes. A week later I returned to the hypnotist and told him I had failed. He put me under again, but nothing happened. He told me, "If this doesn't work, we'll try psychoanalysis."

I was forty before I smoked a cigarette, about the time the surgeon general issued his fuddy-duddy warning. I was a college teacher, separated from my wife, and had entered a fringe of the counterculture that took over the sixties. My students' greatest sport was to turn a professor on. Never did I need to buy a joint, and unlike Bill Clinton I accepted instruction in inhaling, learning to enjoy the pain. Alas, I had another, deeper reason for seeking humiliation and harm. I endured a volcanic love affair with a beautiful young woman who was not psychotic but whose utterance sounded like surrealism. She had other attractions, of which she was aware, but she felt devastated by one unforgivable flaw: she could not stop smoking Kents. In our assignations the foggy air trembled with erotic joy. She adored our sex but abhorred her own fog. Then, viciously, she dumped me. I went crazy, I daydreamed suicide, I took up Kents for revenge. I have not seen her for decades, and at eighty-some I am still proclaiming, "*Look what you did!*"

If my tender father had not smoked so much, by now he would have turned one hundred and fifteen. From the late sixties into the millennium, American living rooms have become smokeless, as well as bars, restaurants, hardware stores, hotel lobbies, cabins, business offices, factory floors, sedans, hospital rooms, pizzerias, sweatshops, town meetings, laboratories, palaces, department stores, supermarkets, barbershops, McDonald's, beauty parlors, art galleries, bookstores, pharmacies, men's rooms, corner groceries, women's rooms, barns except for mine, movie houses, dairies, airports, offices of thoracic surgeons, depots, tearooms, Automats, cafeterias, town halls, Macy's, gymnasiums, igloos, waiting rooms, museums, newsrooms, classrooms, steel mills, libraries, lecture halls, emergency rooms, auditoriums, parks, Mongolian yurts, beaches, and definitely funeral parlors.

Physical Malfitness

MY TRAINER, PAMELA SANBORN, works me out Tuesday and Thursday afternoons. She's tiny and strong, four foot ten and a hundred pounds of muscle. If she had to, I'm sure she could carry my two hundred pounds slung over her shoulders. For half an hour each session she has me do cardio on the treadmill, squat with five-pound weights, lift tenners over my head and out from my sides, stretch muscles, stand up no hands with a beach ball between my knees, and do push-ups (as it were) standing against a wall. Exercise hurts, as well it might, since by choice and for my pleasure I didn't do it for eighty years. (Once in my fifties I walked four miles.) Pam is cute and loves to work out. When her marriage ended, she found a new companion on an Internet site called Fitness Singles. At the moment, the two of them are bicycling through Italy.

When I divorced, I looked for women who lazed around after poetry readings.

. . .

Exercise is boring. Everything is boring that does not happen in a chair (reading and writing) or in bed. Sculptors and painters and musicians live longer than writers, who exercise only their fingers with pen or on a keyboard. Sculptors chisel or weld or mold clay. Painters work standing up. They drink quarts of cognac every night but return to physical activity the next morning. A tuba player holds a weighty object and breathes deeply. Even a harmonica requires more fitness than writing.

People have tried to encourage my mobility. Jane for years cherished cats. This house is full of Jane's cat presents from friends — cat night-lights and cat doorstops and cat china dolls. In time she found herself mooning after dogs at the house of a writer friend. When she adopted Gus, Jane (who called me Perkins) invented an excuse: "It will get Perkins off his ass." Thus for several years I walked fifteen minutes a day. The husband of a friend, who went dog walking with me, swears that I parked the car on a dirt road, let Gus out to walk alone, and whistled him back. Then Jane died of leukemia, the dog's hindquarters failed, and my hindquarters failed. I sit on my ass all day, writing in longhand, which Kendel types up. Sometimes in a car I would pass Pancake Road, two miles away, and see a man walking his collie, the dog stepping out on his forepaws, two wheels harnessed to his backside. These days I no longer drive past Pancake Road or anywhere. I push wheels ahead of me instead of pulling them behind me like the dog. With my forepaws holding the handles of a four-wheeled roller, my buckling hindquarters slowly shove my carcass forward. I drool as I walk, and now and then I sniff a tree.

· · ·

I have been told that as a baby I crawled up on a kitchen table and devoured a quarter pound of butter. I spewed it out quickly, and mouth-memory has endured in my distaste for yellow milk-fat. Because it was so athletic to climb the table, perhaps my misadventure also led to my athletic malfitness. Or maybe it came from my mother Lucy. On the farm as a girl, she didn't chop trees or hayfields or haul ice from the pond. With her mother Kate she helped wash overalls, squeeze clothes through a mangle, and hang them out to dry. She carried cans of corn and peas up from the root cellar to the kitchen. Otherwise she was not a muscular sort. Her mother mopped the hardwood kitchen floor every night while Lucy studied Latin for the mill town high school. Later, they sat under an oil lamp while they knitted, tatted, and darned socks. Everything my mother did was useful and her hands were nimble, but nothing my mother did stretched a tendon, nothing firmed a muscle.

Upstairs in the back chamber, where everything goes when it dies — a green rocking chair with a broken rocker, long-dead long underwear, oil lamps retired after electricity — I found a pair of wooden skis with runners two inches thick, heavy as a hayload, on which I was told my mother slid down a slope. Her lift had to be a horse that trudged uphill as she hung on to a rope. When I moved into the farmhouse in middle age, I decided to try cross-country skis. I bought a pair, and in a flat field next to the barn I stood up and fell down, stood up and fell down, stood up and fell down. I retired the skis to the back chamber. With snowshoes I didn't fall down so much, but it was harder getting up. I did not try ice skates.

. . .

My father remembered skating on January ponds, playing short-stop, even running sprints at school. In Hamden he and I played catch on Greenway Street and I threw the baseball over his head. He trotted up the pavement to retrieve it. *Trotted.* We played ping-pong in the cellar, and it wasn't until he started shaking that I beat him two out of three games. Every Saturday morning he golfed with his foursome. He acquired his golfing passion when he caddied for spare change as a boy. As a grownup he became a member of the New Haven Country Club and hired his own caddies. When my parents were first married, my father tried to teach my mother golf. She found it hard to hit that little white ball with that long wooden stick. Once when my father walked a few yards in front of her, my mother's golf ball flew up the fairway past him. He turned around, ecstatic, to congratulate her on her drive. She didn't tell him right away that she had thrown it.

I did not love golf. Sometimes on a family ride we would stop at a driving range. My mother would sit on a bench as my father bought two pails of exhausted golf balls and we stood at a rubber tee and swung away. Mostly I missed, or tapped the ball three inches, but occasionally I caught it flush and it rose majestically into the air and landed a graceful thirty-seven yards downrange. There was a target two hundred yards beyond it.

I wasn't any good playing anything. Back in Spring Glen Grammar School, a physical education instructor came on Tuesdays and brought two basketballs and set us into circles — one for people who had passed a basketball before, another for those who hadn't. I had touched a basketball on a Saturday at the YMCA, so I stood in the Circle of Experience. After one or two rounds our instructor switched me to the Circle of Innocence.

By the time I moved on to Hamden High School the war had started. Everyone expected to be drafted shortly after graduation, so physical education amped up its requirements. We boxed. My opponent was a quiet, willowy guy and our fists mangled only the sweaty air of the gym. In spring we were required to run a quarter mile, which I mostly walked. Still, I lost my breath.

Doubtless that's why, when I switched to Exeter after tenth grade, I went out for cross-country. As I did laps for endurance, I heard my eighty-year-old coach — the war had resurrected elderly faculty — mutter, "Truck horse." My feelings were hurt. I worked on improving my style, but when I ran cross-country, agony rotated from ribs of one side to ribs of the other. I faked turning my ankle.

Summers on the farm I hayed with my grandfather. I milked cows badly, I was scared to pull eggs from underneath hens, but I liked haying. I liked sitting up front with my grandfather behind the slow old horse as we approached the hayfield. Even more I loved the slower plod back to the barn. My grandfather told story after story with affection and humor. Sometimes he recited wonderful, terrible poems he had memorized for school. Loading the rack with hay took more muscle than sitting and listening to stories, but I tolerated the strain. My grandfather, as he approached and passed seventy, stuck his pitchfork into a pile of hay and raised it over his head onto the hayrack, where I hauled it into place and treaded it down, so that interlocked forkfuls would not slide off while we plodded back home. The air inside the barn was intolerably hot and chaffy. My grandfather by himself pitched the load up to the lofts, where it would remain until winter brought the cattle inside. Meantime I rested in the cool of the living room.

When I was sixteen, I found a girlfriend in Connecticut and stopped haying. To pay for rum and Cokes at a teenage tavern, I found a summer job where I could sit down.

It was the wrist skill of Ping-Pong that budged me toward athletic triumph. At prep school I learned squash, where I could snap the ball with my table tennis wrists. Although the playing space was large, the rackets reached long and I delayed between points to breathe. When I got to college I tried out for the freshman team. One by one the hackers were cut, often with generous words from the young coach. Then came my one athletic triumph: I was the last man cut from the freshman squash squad at Harvard.

In Ann Arbor, when I taught, I never lost cellar ping-pong games. My prowess went to my head, and when the Ann Arbor Table Tennis Association printed a notice in the paper, I called and asked to join. "Are you a beginner or a moderate?" said a voice. I hemmed and hawed out of modesty and was told I was a beginner. We played on adjacent basketball courts where we could retreat twenty feet behind the table to retrieve a slam. I was a beginner.

Baseball has always been my favorite sport to follow. I could never play it. I tried and tried. I arrived at the University of Michigan as a twenty-six-year-old assistant professor without a graduate degree. The *Michigan Daily* told me that the English department softball team was to play against Physics at two p.m. on a Saturday. Interested students and teachers might participate. I found myself on an intramural field among a host of grad students. I was chosen — however skeptical the scholars-in-training — to play left field and bat ninth. In the second inning, before I had a chance to strike out, a fly ball approached me in the field. I kept a steady eye as I moved under it and poised my glove. The ball hit me straight on the skull. My teammates gathered around me until I staggered up and was replaced by a burly medievalist. When I collapsed on the bench, a woman approached me, saying that she was a nurse. If later I felt nauseated or had double vision, she advised me to hasten to an emergency room.

Baseball is for watching. From April to October I watch the Red Sox every night. (Other sports fill the darker months.) I do not write; I do not work at all. After supper I become the American male — but I think I do something else. Try to forgive my comparisons, but before Yeats went to sleep every night he read an American Western. When Eliot was done with poetry and editing, he read a mystery book. Everyone who concentrates all day, in the evening needs to let the half-wit out for a walk. Sometimes it is Zane Grey, sometimes Agatha Christie, sometimes the Red Sox.

As I entered my mid-seventies, my legs weakened and it became treacherous to walk on uneven ground. I decided that if I were to survive, I should do something. I bought a stationary bike and set it up in front of the television. Watching Ken Burns's *Civil War* on tape, I managed to pump for seven minutes each day, until I fell trying to climb down from the machine, which in its turn fell on me and knocked out a tooth. I gave the bike away and bought a treadmill that was too big for the television room. In my bedroom I walked at two miles an hour listening to NPR. Each afternoon I did four minutes, sometimes even five, before sagging into bottomless boredom in spite of NPR. It was my doctor who told me about the Hogan Fitness Center at Colby-Sawyer College, only fifteen minutes away, which was Pam's domain. Twice a week I parked outside, took an elevator upstairs to avoid climbing steps, and delivered myself to Pam in a gym cluttered with barbells and exercise machines. Twice a week we walked together around a wooden track for cardio's fifteen minutes. We talked. Then for another fifteen minutes I attempted fitness and balance. Balance was a major problem. Pam showed me how to stand up when I fell down.

When I was eighty my second car wreck stopped my driving and I handed my license to a state trooper. At home when I caught my breath, I telephoned Pam at the fitness center and told her, sobbing, that I could never see her again. Others could shop for me, or take me to the doctor's, but who would drive me to the gym twice a week, hang around for half an hour, and drive me back? Pam calmed me down, saying that she would come to me. Thus Pam drives to my house twice a week at three-thirty p.m., bringing weights and straps and curved plastic platforms where I can practice losing balance. I accomplish fifteen minutes on the treadmill. I stand up from the bed with a horse collar full of sand draped around my neck as we try to fend off the wheelchair. With Pam I am able to exercise without boredom because I love her and talk to her all the time. For sixty years I have been writing my autobiography in book after book, poetry and prose, but Pam does not read autobiography, so I repeat all my stories. Sometimes I choose topics — Famous Writers I Have Known; My Athletic Career — but mostly I remain chronological, beginning with stories of my parents, who met when they attended Bates College, through my birth, through infancy and eating butter, through childhood and grammar school . . . Often when we have finished our workout, Pam takes notes on my daily achievements in malfitness, then adds a reminder of where we are in the story. When she returns from Italy we will still be at Oxford in 1952, and I will tell her about sitting at my desk typing in the frigid January of Christ Church College. At the top of her notes she has written, "He cuts fingertip off glove."

Dr. Dr. Dr. Dr. Dr. Dr. Dr. Dr. Dr. Dr.

AN OP-ED IN the *Boston Globe,* remarking on near-corpses who keep on doing what they've always done, compared me to Mick Jagger. Never before had I been so honored. The columnist mentioned others: Keith Richards, Alice Munro, and William Trevor, who was born the year I was. At seventy, Jagger is a juvenile among us eighty-five-year-olds — but his face as he jumps and gyrates resembles something retrieved from a bog.

Some honors honor. Some dishonors dishonor; some honors more or less dishonor. Grace and disgrace. Professional and personal. Disaster and survival.

It's all bragging. My pursuit of honor started early. When I was a boy there was a popular radio show called *Quiz Kids,* where young geniuses — eight years to twelve? — sat around a table with microphones and answered complicated questions from a host. "Name the nations and colonies that border the Mediterranean Sea." Maybe it was a fraud, like television quiz shows later. This enterprise published a monthly, *Quiz Kids Magazine,* with a column of letters from boys and girls about their avocations. I was twelve and got a dollar for my letter about my hobby of writing poetry. The check was a big deal — my weekly allowance was fifty cents — but the honor of publication was monumental. My hobby turned into my profession.

It's personal dishonor to spend a night in jail, especially for a crime as vulgar as DUI. One morning in Michigan, a year after my divorce, my girlfriend telephoned to cancel our excursion to New York. She hadn't slept all night. She feared her boyfriend would find out about us. She resisted my jocular entreaties and my frantic ones, and when I turned nasty she hung up in rage. I swallowed a diet spansule at eight a.m., which would keep me alert and speedy all day, and drove to a bar in the country. It was isolated, sleazy, and opened early. I ordered beer by the pitcher, and finished three before returning to Ann Arbor, where I struggled from bar to bar. My belly swollen with gallons of Heineken and Amstel, I may have eaten a hamburger by midnight, when I decided it was time to drive home. I walked back carefully, lurching, and as I opened the car door a police cruiser pulled up beside me. "Don't drive, buddy." Immediately I understood the policeman's benign advice. "Oh, thank you, officer. I'm much obliged. Thank you."

I started walking home, only a mile away, planning to wake early and retrieve my Plymouth. Then I suffered one of those flashes of intuition common to people who have drunk beer for sixteen hours. *The night air has cleared my head! Of course I can drive!* With my right wheels in the gutter, I wobbled at five miles an hour and the same policeman arrested me. I spent the night in jail and lost my license for three months. At least I learned something. The drunk tank was outfitted with bunks of sheet steel. It was a Friday night and all bunks were occupied. On the concrete floor I sprawled out among others, and dozed in five-minute stretches until the bone pain woke me up. During the night, a generous bunker departed his metal mattress and tapped me on the shoulder. A sheet of steel, as I discovered, was soft as lamb's wool compared to concrete.

When you read the back flap of a book of poems, or a contributor's note for a short story, or hear the introduction to a writer reading his work, the list of honors is interminable. We hear of first book prizes, second book prizes, prizes named for writers who won earlier prizes (there is a Donald Hall Prize), as well as medals and fellowships and residencies. It is even noted when writers were short-listed for something they didn't win. My favorite is "Nominated for the Pulitzer Prize." Each year a panel of three poet-outsiders lists three candidates from a thousand nominees and sends their names to the Pulitzer people. Once I was a panelist, and my house filled with boxes of deplorable books *nominated* — because anybody can nominate anybody for a Pulitzer. In Michigan I knew two young poets, untalented pals who published each other and nominated each other regularly for the Pulitzer Prize. Their book jackets noted the honor.

Like an idiot, I was flattered at first to get honorary degrees. Donors to a college receive most unearned doctorates, but academic institutions try to cover their fundraising by decorating a few cultural or political figures. I sweated in cap and gown under the sun hearing graduates' names pompously uttered. I sat beside governmental stars and we chattered about politics while ex-students crossed a stage shaking hands and clutching certificates. When cheers rang out for a sorority queen or a football captain, we middle-aged honorees clapped and dehydrated. But I was not running for office, and I wearied of accepting doctorates, dishonored by honor. Upstairs there remains a hat rack of gowns topped with caps beside a table holding dusty diplomas. The poet Geoffrey Hill has addressed me as "Dr. Dr. Dr. Dr. Dr. Dr. Dr. Dr. Dr. Dr."

I claim it an honor that in 1975 I gave up lifetime tenure, medical expenses, and a pension in exchange for forty joyous years of freelance writing. One children's book won a Caldecott, and will stay in print after the rest of my things are no longer available. I wrote poetry, but not for monetary reward. For mortgage and food I produced magazine pieces about baseball and New Hampshire. I could not do it now. Only the *New Yorker* remains among magazines that pay enough to notice. *Esquire* and the *Atlantic* and *Harper's* begin to collapse like *Godey's Lady's Book*. Well, *Playboy* survives. The good thing is that *Playboy* pays; the bad thing is that no one reads it.

Perpetual falling down is not a dishonor so much as a disadvantage. On a day when Jane was alive I took Gus for a walk. He wrapped his leash around me and I fell face-first in the driveway's gravel. I put the dog back in the house, wrapped a towel around my cheeks, wrote Jane a note — she was lunching with a friend — and drove to Emergency as the towel sopped up blood.

When Dr. Yuskaitis had removed one hundred and forty-seven specks of gravel from my face, grappling with his sterile tweezers, he remarked, "How tedious." Ten years after Jane died, I met Linda at a church supper poetry reading. The day before, I had fallen over an ottoman to crack my ribs and blacken my eye. Another time I was running to the car to drive with Linda to a restaurant and my right foot tripped over a brick. "It's okay," I said. "It doesn't hurt. Let's go to Piero's." I was interrupted by blood flowing down my face, and we sped to Emergency. Linda was appalled. It was a pity to miss Piero's *luganiga,* but at least I got a free haircut and a set of stitches. Once in an airport I carefully sat down, waiting for luggage, on a bench that was not there. In Manhattan I emerged from a theater with my daughter and her family. I was running away from *The Lion King* and scrambled behind a woman who unfortunately dragged a suitcase. A crowd gathered. A woman shouted, "Get him a Pepsi!" Which seemed strange until I noticed that my face was ballooning.

These falls happened before I became disabled.

Some honors get more attention than others. When I visited the White House and the President hung a medal around my neck, my local newspaper ran a story on the front page. No one else noticed. On the other hand, there was the announcement that I would become Poet Laureate of the United States. A week later a New Hampshire Public Radio interviewer asked me how it felt to be appointed Poet Laureate. I told her, "Devastated." I was molested by letters, telephone calls, and interviews. Three television companies occupied my farm. (Only PBS was friendly and smart.) Radio stations pushed microphones into my face. I had visits from the *Boston Globe,* the *Los Angeles Times,* the *Washington Post,* and the *Concord Monitor.* Many journalists brought cameramen, and *Sports Illustrated* pictured me with my grandfather's bat on my shoulder. The *New York Times* noticed my appointment below the fold and later added an op-ed. The *Wall Street Journal* did two pieces, a news item and a glittering essay. My appointment as Laureate even crossed the ocean. "J.C.," who writes the back-page column for the *Times Literary Supplement,* recorded my appointment with approval and quoted from a *TLS* poem of mine I didn't remember.

After weeks of chatter and overattention, I ran away with Linda to silence at Ipanema in Brazil. When we returned to New Hampshire a stranger in a restaurant — with a beehive hairdo — ordered me a napoleon. Later, I was a useless Laureate.

Like everyone at eighty, I assumed that I was a good driver. Kendel had cut clippings from a newspaper offering refresher courses for senior drivers, but I was too busy. (Maybe she had noticed something?) In May I drove to New London to buy some sausages. As I drove back I was smoking a cigarette. It dropped from my hand to the car's floor and I reached down to pick it up. My fingers could not feel the butt, so I took a peek. The next thing I remember is the compression of my seat belt and the thud of a slow-moving head-on collision. The car I had struck dropped its engine to the pavement. I looked for victims. An ambulance sirened up to attend to dismemberment and death, which thank goodness had not happened. The couple in the car I hit staggered out intact, and I approached them to apologize. "I'm sorry. It's my fault." The man had an epiphany. "Are you Donald Hall?

I've always wanted to meet you." I answered, "Sorry to bump into you this way." He didn't laugh at my joke.

Friends happened by and helped me home. The car was towed to the body shop on Pancake Road, where Jeff Sanborn put it together again. Weeks later, the Wilmot policeman stopped by with a ticket.

In August of the same year I did it again, although I no longer smoked while driving. This time I was criminally impatient. I left my house at six or six-thirty to get the paper and a breakfast sandwich. It was raining hard, a thunderstorm, as I drove to the Circle K. When I came out, the rain was harder and I rushed into my Honda. Impetuously I pulled out onto Route 11 while the thunderstorm thickened. I could not see the pavement. I was moving slowly — not drunk, not reaching for a cigarette — in search of a fence to the right, thinking I could scrape against it and stop. Then I felt the now-familiar zap of a low-speed collision. The rainburst stopped and the sun came out. I stared ahead at the compact car mating with my Honda. I had somehow meandered to the *left*-hand side of the road.

Another car had hit the rear of the car I hit. How many people dialed 911 on their cell phones? Ambulances arrived, police cars, fire trucks. At first I could not open my door, but someone came with a crowbar. Again I hadn't killed anybody. A sensible, depressing thought settled in: *I will never drive again.* A state trooper held out his hand and I gave him my license.

My childhood hometown threw a bash to celebrate my last book of poems, shortly before my eighty-third birthday. Except for summers on the farm, I grew up in a Connecticut suburb in the house where my mother survived to be ninety. Jane and I drove to see her every month when she could no longer drive, and after she died I thought that Hamden was over. I didn't know anyone there — and so I was surprised to be asked to a tribute from the town, sponsored by the Hamden library. I was amazed and ecstatic that four hundred people came. There was an introduction, anecdotes, and poems from the Connecticut Poetry Society. It went on and on. Then I read some poems and took a few questions. Afterward, fifty people surrounded me, saying, "My mother taught you French!" "My grandfather worked for your grandfather!" "Your father gave me this book with his own hands!" and "Do you remember me?" I did not recognize my date for the prom.

At my birthday, back in New Hampshire, my children and grandchildren gathered for dinner at a restaurant's long table. I was so excited about the Hamden occasion that I described it to the left side of the table, then turned right and repeated everything. "I don't know why," I said, "but it pleased me as much as the White House." My beautiful and sharp granddaughter Allison said, "Maybe it was because you were the only one."

Including the dropped cigarette that occasioned my first automobile accident, I have fumbled cigarettes ten thousand times, and long ago renounced the pleasure of smoking in bed. I sucked on most of my cigarettes as I sat reading in the overstuffed blue armchair, the same one from which I looked out the window at winter birds. One time when Kendel was visiting, she noticed that the carpet between my chair and a low bookshelf was burned away, as were the backs of some books. She was horrified when I told her that I had dropped a cigarette and couldn't find it. She begged me — no, she commanded me — to telephone her if I couldn't find a dropped cigarette. I didn't want to wake her up in the night, but she would not let me go until I promised, so I promised.

Often I go to bed at ten-thirty. I sleep for an hour or so, then wake feeling jumpy and sit up for a while, reading a magazine and smoking. Shortly after promising Kendel, I dropped a cigarette in my overstuffed chair. I could not find it! I felt horrible, because I had promised her and it was midnight. I pulled out the cushions of the chair. Nothing. Then I reached down below the cushion line and found it. I finished inhaling the ember and went back to bed. I slept soundly until about three a.m., when the blast of a siren awakened me. I looked at my alarm clock, groggy, as if it could make such a noise. I sat on the side of the bed, two-thirds asleep, aghast to listen to the blast — then woke enough to see smoke billowing through the bedroom door. The screech was the smoke alarm! I had the brains to push the button around my neck. The voice asked gently, "Are you all right?" "Smoke is filling my bedroom!" "Stay where you are!" In a short while, after alerting firemen and an ambulance, the voice came back, "Don't move. Is your front door unlocked?"

Firemen from Wilmot and nearby towns arrived with a twenty-four-hour ambulance from New London. Kendel joined us, alerted by the button people. The front door crashed open and the ambulance crew carried me outside on a stretcher through the smoke. I saw no flame — but my big blue chair was pouring out a thick column of smoke. Confused as I was, I had glimpsed the source of the conflagration. The cigarette I found in my chair at midnight, alight enough to smoke, had left behind in the chair's bowels a burning hunk of tobacco. In the ambulance the crew confirmed that I was intact. They took my blood pressure over and over, lower every time. It was a warm November night, but it was November. Kendel took shelter in the ambulance. At her request, they took her blood pressure also.

On my front lawn the blue chair stood soaked and looking lonely. In the house the firemen opened the windows and blew the smoke outdoors, downstairs and up. When the ambulance crew took me back inside I could not smell a whiff. I had been saved by the shriek of the alarm that my friend Carole Colburn had thought to install ten years ago. Two weeks ago Linda had checked it out when it made a noise like an insect. She replaced the dying battery. Women had saved me again. Cigarettes are not only a dishonor but lethal, and not only on account of lung cancer. Was my life in danger from smoke inhalation? I think so. In the morning the armchair on the lawn again billowed dense smoke. The firemen had put it out only temporarily, and it recovered its prodigious outpouring. Kendel arrived and dialed 911. "This is not an emergency." Firemen returned with water and foam, but they needed to use axes to chop the blue armchair into smokeless shreds.

Death

IT IS SENSIBLE of me to be aware that I will die one of these days. I will not *pass away*. Every day millions of people *pass away*—in obituaries, death notices, cards of consolation, e-mails to the corpse's friends—but people don't *die*. Sometimes they rest in peace, quit this world, go the way of all flesh, depart, give up the ghost, breathe a last breath, join their dear ones in heaven, meet their Maker, ascend to a better place, succumb surrounded by family, return to the Lord, go home, cross over, or leave this world. Whatever the fatuous phrase, death usually happens peacefully (asleep) or after a courageous struggle (cancer). Sometimes women lose their husbands. (Where the hell did I put him?) Some expressions are less common in print: push up the daisies, kick the bucket, croak, buy the farm, cash out. All euphemisms conceal how we gasp and choke turning blue.

Cremation hides the cadaver; ashes preclude rot. Neanderthals and *Homo sapiens* stuck their dead underground or in mounds. Pyramids sealed up pharaohs. Romans shifted by the century between incineration and burial. Commonly Hindus burnt dead bodies by the Ganges, in the old days performing *sati* by adding a live widow to the pyre. Cinders clogged the river, along with dead babies of families too poor to buy wood. Zoroastrians and Tibetans tended to raise corpses onto platforms for vultures to eat. My favorite anecdote of ash disposal is recent. After I finished a poetry reading, a generous admirer presented me a jar of her late husband's remains.

Myself, I'll be a molderer, like my wife Jane.

At some point in my seventies, death stopped being interesting. I no longer checked out ages in obituaries. Earlier, if I was fifty-one and the cadaver was fifty-three, for a moment I felt anxious. If the dead man was fifty-one and I was fifty-three, I felt relief. If a person lives into old age, there's a moment when he or she becomes eldest in the family, perched on top of a hill as night rises. My mother at ninety left me the survivor. Soon I will provide that honor to my son. When he was born, I was twenty-five and wrote a poem called "My Son My Executioner." A decade ago I went to the emergency room when I fell and hurt myself. It was no big deal. The resident doctor dropped by and we chatted. When I asked about blood pressure numbers, he said I had nothing to worry about. "How many years do you want to live anyway?" Without thinking I grabbed a number out of the air. "Oh, until eighty-three," I told him. On my eighty-fourth birthday I was quietly relieved.

In my eighties, the days have narrowed as they must. I live on one floor eating frozen dinners. Louise the postwoman brings letters to my porch, opens the door, and tosses the mail on a chair. I get around — bedroom, bathroom, kitchen, new chair by the window, electrical reclining (or lifting) chair for Chris Matthews and baseball — by spasming from one place to another pushing a four-wheeled roller. I try not to break my neck. I write letters, I take naps, I write essays.

The people I love will mourn me, but I won't be around to commiserate. I become gloomy thinking of insensate things I will leave behind. My survivors will cram into plastic bags the tchotchkes I have lived with, expanding a landfill. I needn't worry about my Andy Warhols. I fret over the striped stone that my daughter picked up at the pond, or my father's desk lamp from college, or a miniature wooden milk wagon from the family dairy. My mother approaching ninety feared that we would junk the Hummel figurines that decorated her mantelpiece, kitsch porcelain dolls popular from the forties to the sixties. Thus, a box of them rests in my daughter's attic. More important to me is this house, which my great-grandfather moved to in 1865 — the family place for almost a century and a half. In the back chamber the generations stored everything broken or useless, because no one knew when they might come in handy. My kids and grandkids don't want to live in rural isolation — why should they? — but it's melancholy to think of the house emptied out. Better it should burn down. Remaining in the old place, I let things go. I shingle the roof, I empty the cesspool, but if a light fixture fails, I do without it. Maybe the next tenant will not want it. I let the old wallpaper flap loose. Somebody will remove four hundred feet of bookshelves.

There are also bits of land I cherish. When Jane and I moved here, we found my great-grandfather's stationery, labeled "Eagle

Pond Farm," and borrowed the name for our address. Last November a friend took me driving past Eagle Pond. It's obscured from my windows by the growth of tall trees, although the pond is only a hundred yards west, twenty-four acres of water. My land includes half the pond's shore. I titled books of essays *Seasons at Eagle Pond* and *Here at Eagle Pond*. Then I collected them as *Eagle Pond*. Then I wrote *Christmas at Eagle Pond*. Back in the day, Jane and I used a tiny, hidden beach, among oak and birch, to lie in the sun on summer afternoons and grill supper on a hibachi. We watched for mink and beaver, we saw the first acorns fall. In the years after she died I visited the pond rarely, and by this time it's long since I've even passed it by. When my friend drove me on its dirt road — an afternoon of bright autumn sunlight, the pond intensely blue with its waters choppy — I glimpsed the birches of our old beach and wept a tear of self-pity.

Of course we start dying when the sperm fucks the egg. (Pro-lifers dwell on this insight.) At my age I feel complacent about death, if sometimes somber, but we all agree that *dying* sucks. I've never been around when somebody, in the middle of a sentence or a sandwich, has the luck to pitch over dead. I've only sat beside two deaths, my grandmother Kate's and my wife Jane's. In both cases the corpse-in-waiting was out of it. Hours earlier each had slipped into Cheyne-Stokes breathing, when the brain stem is stubborn about retaining oxygen though the big brain has departed. Cheyne-Stokes is one long breath followed by three quick ones, then a pause. The brain stem holds on, in my experience, for as long as twelve hours. Because my grandmother's mouth drooped open and looked sore, a nurse spooned water on her red tongue. She choked as if she had swallowed the wrong way. I held her hand. I rubbed Jane's head until the long breath ceased. Least enviable are folks who die while alive, panicked as they rush, still conscious, from pink to blue. My father and my mother both died alive.

Beginning as a schoolboy, death turned me on, and for decades I practiced an enthusiastic morbidity. At home a whole bunch of great-aunts and -uncles took their turns at dying. At ten I enjoyed banquets of precocious lamentation, telling myself that Death had become a reality. In seventh grade I wrote my first poem, which explained that Death hunted you down, screeching through the night, until Death called your name. When I was fifteen, more and more practicing the poet, I decided that if I announced that I would die young, it would appeal to cheerleaders. I let it be known that I would die between pages seventeen and eighteen, not noticing that seventeen and eighteen are two sides of the same page. When I started writing real poems I kept to the subject, though death dropped its capital letter. I wrote cheerful poems — about farm horses or a family dog — and pointed out that eventually they all died. Who would have guessed? I wrote a poem, "In Praise of Death," that tried to get rid of death by flattery.

Except in print, I no longer dwell on it. It's almost relaxing to know I'll die fairly soon, as it's a comfort not to obsess about my next orgasm. I've been ambitious, and ambition no longer has plans for the future — except these essays. My goal in life is making it to the bathroom. In the past I was often advised to live in the moment. Now what else can I do? Days are the same, generic

93

and speedy—I seem to remove my teeth shortly after I glue them in—and weeks are no more tedious than lunch. They elapse and I scarcely notice. The only boring measure is the seasons. Year after year they follow the same order. Why don't they shake things up a bit? Start with summer, followed by spring, winter, then maybe Thanksgiving?

I've wanted to kill myself only three times, each on account of a woman. Two of them dumped me and the other died. Each time, daydreams of suicide gave me comfort. My father presented me with a .22 Mossberg when I was twelve, but self-assassination by .22 is chancy. If I didn't aim it like a surgeon, I could spend the rest of my life on a breathing machine. My friend Bruno suggested an infallible method—to carry my gun into Eagle Pond, wading up to my knees, then plonk a long-rifle bullet into my head. I would drown if the shot didn't finish me off. Bruno gave suicide a lot of thought, and he took no chance with himself. In his Beverly Hills condo he pulled the pin on a hand grenade clutched to his chest.

By this time, even if I wanted to, I'm too frail and wobbly to walk into Eagle Pond.

In middle life I came close to dying of natural causes. When I was sixty-one I had colon cancer, deftly removed, but two years later it metastasized to my liver. A surgeon removed half of that organ and told me I might live five years. Both Jane and I assumed I would die soon, and she massaged me every day, trying to rub the cancer out. I went through the motions of chemo and finished writing what I was able to finish. Aware of my own approaching death, I was astonished and appalled when Jane came down with leukemia. Her death at forty-seven — I was sixty-six — was not trivial. Six years later I had a small stroke and my potential death felt matter-of-fact. A carotid artery was eighty-five percent occluded. Dr. Harbaugh removed a pencil-wide, inch-long piece of plaque during a two-hour operation under local anesthetic. I enjoyed hearing the chitchat of the white-coated gang. Now and then somebody asked me to squeeze a dog's ball, which tinkled to affirm my consciousness. I was disappointed when Dr. Harbaugh wouldn't let me take the obstruction back home.

In his "Homage to Sextus Propertius," Ezra Pound has his poet protagonist say, "I shall have, doubtless, a boom after my funeral." Particular circumstances contribute to the response, like death at a comparatively young age. When Jane died, obituaries reprinted her poems. I was interviewed about her. NPR rebroadcast her interview with Terry Gross. In India — Jane and I had visited — there were ceremonies in her honor in Bombay, New Delhi, and Madras. There were memorials in New Hampshire, in New York, at Harvard, and in Minneapolis. When her posthumous selected poems, *Otherwise,* came out on the first anniversary of her death, it quickly went into three hardback printings. Eighteen months later a paperback flourished, and her publishers have now added a *Complete Poems.* I love her work — but her books sold as they first did because of leukemia and her age. Eighteen years later she is reprinted in anthologies. Maybe she'll stick around.

My dearest old friend just died at eighty-nine. At least he died at home. I'm old enough to remember when everybody died in their houses, tended by family as Jane was tended. I was nine when I spent a summer at the farm while my grandmother's older sister lay dying in the parlor. Parlors in those days were reserved for special events — entertaining the pastor, funerals, weddings, and dying. (The parlor has become the television room.) Great-Aunt Nannie lay on a cot, blind, unable to turn over in bed, her back in continuous pain. She told my grandparents Kate and Wesley that the people of this house (Kate and Wesley) tortured her by making her sleep on a woodpile. She told Kate that she wanted to see her family, and Kate told her that she could arrange a visit from Kate and Wesley. When Kate and Wesley dropped by, Aunt Nannie was overjoyed. She died soon after I left for school, in September 1938, just before the New England hurricane. My mother got stuck coming back from the funeral.

Some fortunate people die in a hospice, which is tender but brief. I visited an old friend, James Wright, as he lay dying in a Bronx hospice, under warm and intelligent care — but the hospice found a bed only four days before he died. My first wife died in a New Hampshire hospice — admitted with six days to live. Some hospitals perform palliative care for the terminally ill. Others of us still die at home, like my father, Jane's father, and two aunts of mine. Jane could have died in a shiny hospital bed but chose home, as I will, if I can manage. In the same bed. These days most old people die in profit-making expiration dormitories. Their loving sons and daughters are busy and don't want to forgo the routine of their lives. One said he would *not* diaper his parents — so he handed them over to women who diapered at the minimum wage. My friend Linda spent two of her college summers working at a place called Eternal Peace, on the three-to-eleven shift. After she fed the patients, she pulled out their teeth and put them in a jar. One night she could not get a woman's teeth out. She pulled and pulled and pulled. One tooth came out dripping blood.

Old folks' storage bins bear encouraging names. I've heard of an Alzheimer's unit called Memory Lane. There are also Pleasant View, Live Forever, Happy Valley, Pastures of Paradise, Paradise Pastures, Heaven's Gate, Peaceful Meadow, Summerglen, Paradise Village Estates, Autumn Wind, Fountain of Youth, Elder Gardens, Harbor Isle, Enchanted Spring, Golden Heirloom, Golden Dawn, Pastures of Plenty, Thistlerock Farm, Village Green, Green Village, Ever Rest, and Everest.

At such an address our elders pass away, or rest in peace, or meet their Maker, or leave this world, or buy the farm . . .

On Rejection and Resurrection

A NOTORIOUS POET sells all fifty poems to magazines, does a book with a publisher's advance, sells out the hardcover and then the paperback. If someone asks the poet to say the poems aloud, one poetry reading brings in more cash than the magazines and books together.

Instead of money, poetry hopes to create beauty, emotion, intelligence, insight, and pleasure all at once, as well as immortality. It rarely does. Whatever their poems try to do, poets are outraged by rejections and editors. (It's well known that the smaller the reward, the fiercer the competition.) Turned down six times by the *New Yorker*, a poet decides, "They don't like me there." Does the poet think that a magazine (which gets a thousand poems a week and publishes two) checks out an index of forbidden names? "No. We don't like *her*." I have a friend who sent a poem to the *New Yorker* that was rejected by e-mail in two and a half hours. He was apoplectic. Did he expect that an editor, or sub-sub-editor, would spend two and a half hours to decide? Rejections often take two and a half minutes. When people send poems to a small magazine and wait a year for rejection, did the editor read over the poem seventeen thousand times? Or did he wait until chagrin overcame boredom? "Damn, I've got to take care of that pile."

My comfort with rejection began by accident, by being fourteen and submitting my poems to the *Atlantic,* the *Nation,* the *New Yorker,* and the *Saturday Review of Literature.* The poems returned with a printed slip. I was briefly disappointed, then found two more long white envelopes—one the stamped, self-addressed one, the other to enclose the same poems—and my juvenile endeavors went out again in the next mail. In minutes I zapped from despair to hope. When I came home from high school, my mother would often greet me cheerfully at the door. "Another rejection today, Donnie."

It's helpful for a poet to be an editor when young, though not so young as fourteen. At Exeter and college I started choosing manuscripts for school magazines, and at Oxford I edited four publications at once. Then I became the first poetry editor of the *Paris Review.* (I knew George Plimpton at college.) I published Geoffrey Hill's poems for the first time, and Robert Bly's, and Thom Gunn's, and in the meantime rejected ten thousand poems and made mistakes. I rejected Allen Ginsberg's "Sunflower Sutra." (He told George I wouldn't know a poem if it buggered me in broad daylight.) Some poems I printed were more humiliating than my dumbest rejections. Still, I learned from editing. There were other ways of writing than the way I had found for myself. I read all the literary magazines, scouting the field. I found friends for life, to whom I later showed my own drafts, with whom I argued usefully. The fellowship of the *Paris Review* — George Plimpton, Peter Matthiessen, William Styron — extended my literary community. At George's parties, at East 72nd Street, I met Philip Roth, Mary McCarthy, Robert Lowell, and Kingsley Amis.

A fellow named Boris visited with a black bag, apparently carrying products not found in drugstores.

As you might guess, not every editorial encounter was benign. Poets' letters arrived for the *Paris Review* saying, "I am the greatest poet alive and if you don't print all my poems you are an asshole." "I am a tenured full professor of English who played offensive tackle in the NFL." "I am a serial murderer." Editors learn not to offer helpful suggestions when they reject a poem. If I hinted that "bouncing baby" might be a cliché, by return mail I heard that I was an idiot, that the metaphor was innovative genius. Bags of poems arrived each month by mail from the office in Paris. Fifty percent I rejected immediately. The first five lines told me that the poem would never do. The better candidates I kept around, reading over and over, sending some back at each rereading. Finally I took maybe one, maybe two. I know I made mistakes. I was arrogant. At the age of twenty-five I felt cheekier about my taste than I have felt in the sixty years after. Probably I was narrower, more dogmatic, and better.

Many years ago I discovered that a good poet, a friend of melancholy temperament, was so devastated by rejection that she could not work on new poems. I argued, but she could not shake her despair. I had an idea. If she would let me, *I* would send her poems out. But if I used my own name, I would seem to be trying to throw my weight around — as if I thought I had weight. I invented Joey Amaryllis, a literary agent who represented only poets, possibly the one poetry agent in the universe. First I rented a post office box at Potter Place, New Hampshire, near where I live but with a different zip code. From the American Stationery Company I ordered letterhead and envelopes with the neonate Joey's address. Writing to editors, Joey was careful to enclose only brisk notes. If Joey told an editor "It's raining today," the editor would suspect that Joey was looking for an angle.

With her permission, I submitted my friend's poems to good magazines, without telling her which ones. When the poems came back, I sent them out again, and when they came back again, I tried again. By agreement I kept quiet when I sent things out, and I never reported a rejection. When an editor took a poem, I spread the joy. One time Joey submitted his client's poems to the editor of an academic quarterly, a man with whom I had a friendly correspondence. Shortly afterward, I happened to write the editor a letter, and without thinking praised my friend. He wrote back that he had recently received poems by this woman, but that they were submitted by somebody else, "and I never read that sort of thing." (The poems had not yet returned to Potter Place.) When I wrote the editor back to confess, and to apologize for my duplicity, he said that my friend should send the poems herself. Decades later, she continues to publish in the same quarterly. Joey also submitted her poems to *Poetry,* which bought several. The editor had printed my own poems, but he made it clear that I annoyed him. Even his notes of acceptance were frosty. On the other hand, he took a shine to Joey Amaryllis, and wrote him warm letters about Joey's generosity.

Why did I undertake this caper? I helped a depressed friend and I promoted good poems. How nice of me. But why did I like it *so much?* I adored being a secret agent. After a couple of years, my friend took over her own marketing and thrived. Joey came in from the cold.

At sixteen, poets think that if they publish in a magazine that will be *it*. When it happens, it is not *it*. Then they think it will be *it* when they publish in *Poetry*. No. The *New Yorker?* No. A book? Good reviews? The Something Prize? A Guggenheim? The National Book Award? The Nobel? No, no, no, no, no, no. Flying back from Stockholm, the Laureate knows that nothing will make *it* certain. The Laureate sighs.

Writers, of course, require praise. After Jane and I moved from Michigan to New Hampshire, I received a thick brown envelope from a cocktail party friend in Ann Arbor, a man who wanted to write novels but who settled for a job in PR. The envelope contained a long, long essay clipped from a literary quarterly in which an unfamiliar professor attacked me for everything I had ever written—my poems, my children's books, a memoir, short stories, even a textbook that the professor's own university had adopted. The professor said that my textbook was good. In fact it was *too good,* and he disparaged my book at length for the manner of its excellence. In a note that accompanied the clipping, my old acquaintance said, "I thought you'd be amused."

Everyone has heard about the Emperor executing the Messenger. The Emperor was right. From the personals in the *New York Review of Books* I hired a hit man.

My generation assumed that the value of an artist proved itself not in contemporary fame but in durability. Lately we have not been hearing much about Robert Lowell, who when he died was at the top of the mountain. We will hear of Lowell again. Will we hear again about his mentor Allen Tate? It can be observed that most poets slide into invisibility, maybe for decades, maybe forever. Andrew Marvell's resurrection took three hundred years. Biographies or collections of letters draw some attention to the poetry, or away from the writing to the writer. So does the manner of death. More people know the lives of John Berryman and Sylvia Plath than know the poetry. Tennyson's glory lasted until the twentieth century decided that no Victorian could be a poet. Yeats died in 1939, and his reputation thrived into the 1960s, an unusually long term. Then his grandiloquence disqualified him. (Jane said that she would not buy a used car from this man.) Yeats will revive as Tennyson did, but not my old teacher Archibald MacLeish, who in his lifetime won three Pulitzer Prizes. So did Robert Frost, but the bulk of Pulitzer Prize winners make a paupers' graveyard. Theodore Roethke, enormously praised in the fifties, became largely invisible by the eighties. I think I see his vast shape looming again at the edge of the shadows. Early death was clearly a successful move by John Keats.

Otherwise we attend to our poets when they are alive — to hear them, to praise them, to despise them, to use them. Death usually removes them. I expect my immortality to expire six minutes after my funeral. Literature is a zero-sum game. One poet revives; another gets deader. Like the Laureate returning from Stockholm, we understand — and we sigh.

Garlic with Everything

WHEN JANE AND I moved to New Hampshire, we often drove to Tilton, where my aunt and uncle lived. On the way, we passed a small white building labeled ITALIAN RESTAURANT, and underneath, repeated on each side of the front door, in letters only slightly smaller: NO GARLIC NO GARLIC.

The declaration did not surprise me. In the old days, New Hampshire's food was almost as ruinous as England's. When I lived summers at my grandparents' farm, haying with my grandfather from 1938 to 1945, my dear grandmother Kate cooked abominably. For noon dinners, we might eat three days of fricasseed chicken from a setting hen that had boiled twelve hours. Sometimes we ate a slice of fried Spam, sometimes sardines. (I puked in the outhouse.) Weekly a butcher parked his truck by the front door and displayed his goods to my grandmother. His roast beef tasted like mummified mule. As for her veggies, they were almost edible. In spring she served fresh parsnips, planted the summer before and harvested when snow melted. She cooked peas and beans fresh all summer. Ball jars preserved vegetables for winter. These pickings from the garden, fresh or canned, came to the table overcooked into mush.

Some things were better. Apples from the root cellar lasted through frost almost until the next crop. Berries became jellies and jams, as cider became vinegar. (A cruet on the dining room table protected us from scurvy.) Three meals a day, at least one pie with an undercooked crust sat on the table. Breakfast was two eggs fried sunny-side up — perfectly fine — and a slice of elderly mince. Henry, the grocer and postmaster down to West Andover, half a mile away, lacked refrigeration, which is why Spam and sardines lined pantry shelves. We had an icebox, which my grandfather daily refreshed with a glassy block from the icehouse. Sometimes I walked down to Henry's to trade a dozen fresh eggs for a roll of toilet paper and a package of salt, or for a can of Spam or sardines. In colder winters of the past, I was told that my ancestors hung a slaughtered hog in the toolshed, removing and melting the lard, cutting pork from the carcass all winter.

We didn't go to restaurants, if there were any, because a horse and buggy limited our range. Sometimes a neighborly Model A drove us to Franklin for shopping. At a counter in Newberry's we could buy a plate of beans and franks for twenty-five cents. For lunch at home I made a raw onion sandwich between slices of Wonder Bread. My grandmother found this new product the miracle of the century. For decades she had made bread — Monday washing, Tuesday ironing, Wednesday baking — and a week later the last loaf resisted the knife and the dentures. Wonder Bread, ten cents a loaf, came to Henry's *already sliced.* Even softer than new-baked bread, it was just as soft a week later, or two weeks. More innovations were yet to appear — Velveeta,

Hostess Twinkies, Miracle Whip — but nothing altered the universe so much as Wonder Bread.

When I went home to Connecticut for the school year, our menu was more sophisticated. Breakfast was Corn Flakes, varied by Wheaties, Cheerios, and Rice Krispies. Milk arrived every morning from the horse cart of my family's Brock-Hall Dairy, delivered to back doors by milkmen who later became route salesmen. I walked home from Spring Glen Grammar School at noon for a peanut butter and jelly sandwich. At night there was something like a lamb chop with canned vegetables and a potato. (When Clarence Birdseye froze peas, his invention required freezers in supermarkets as enormous as tennis courts.) A favorite dish in Hamden was American chop suey, which my mother continued to fabricate when she was ninety. Melt a quarter pound of butter in a frying pan. Chop an onion and sizzle it. Add half a pound of crumbled hamburger. Add a whole can of Chef Boy-Ar-Dee and serve. Butter, onions, and hamburger stirred together with depraved pseudo-Italian spaghetti had nothing to do with chop suey. (Chop suey had nothing to do with China.) It was American haute cuisine.

On September twentieth every year I got to choose my menu — meatloaf, corn niblets, and rice were followed by candles on chocolate cake with vanilla icing and a scoop of Brock-Hall ice cream. Some kind of dessert followed every meal, often tapioca pudding ("fish eyes and glue") or Jell-O chilled into molds with tasty canned fruit. It sounds like a lot of work for my mother, but cooking was almost all she did. In suburban Connecticut, middle-class women were required to stay at home and do nothing but cook and iron. Housecleaning was for immigrants. My mother played bridge, belonged to women's clubs, and shopped. She washed and ironed fourteen white shirts a week; dress clothes were required for father and son.

Sunday nights we ate sandwiches at a small rolling table next to the radio while we listened to Jack Benny at six p.m. The program was half an hour long, followed by Phil Harris and then Fred Allen. (Sometimes an hour later I heard Bing Crosby on a forbidden portable radio under my bedroom blanket.) The sandwiches were processed cheese spread on Wonder Bread with the crusts cut off and each sandwich split in half. The cheese came in little Kraft glasses — pineapple and cream cheese, pimento and orange cheese spread. When they were empty, the little glasses, smaller at the bottom and wider at the top, could hold our canned orange juice. In New Hampshire my grandmother used cheese glasses from Hamden for her bedtime tipple of warm Moxie.

In Connecticut on special occasions we went out to eat at a restaurant on Long Island Sound called the Sea Shell. My dinner began with shrimp cocktail — three shrimp in ketchup and horseradish — then tenderloin steak with potato and a vegetable. For dessert I picked from displays in a cart — chocolate cake, sugared strawberries — and the three courses cost ninety-nine cents. (Grampa recites prices in order to shock the young. "Gas cost a dollar for five gallons, with a set of dishes if you filled the tank.") Mostly we ate at home — the Betty Crocker diet, which, like New Hampshire's 1975 Italian restaurant, did not include garlic.

Going to Hamden High School I discovered garlic. Spring Glen Grammar School was suburban middle class and pale. At Hamden High I first heard "Paisan!" shouted from one friend to another. In the decades between the wars, immigrants by the thousands arrived from Calabria and Sicily. Our basketball team was composed of set-shooters who averaged five foot two. As I joined the society of Hamden High, I rejected Spring Glen's culture because it sniffed at people with accents. I hung out with friends who were second-generation Italians, and they altered my diet. In pizza joints I began my romance with garlic. It's hard to believe, but at that time pizza was exotic. In most American cities there were no places that served pizza, much less chains of Pizza Huts, Domino's, Papa Gino's, Pizza Chefs, and Little Caesars. Except in southern-Italian neighborhoods, pizza was unknown coast to coast. Even in northern Italy people didn't know pizza. In 1951 I asked for pizza in a Florentine restaurant. The waiter was puzzled. He disappeared into the kitchen, and when he came back he told me I could have it tomorrow. Did the chef find it in a cookbook? The next day he brought me the worst pizza I have ever eaten — pasty, doughy, tasteless except for garlic. I am told that Florence has pizza parlors now.

In Hamden we ate Italian whenever the boys and I spent a night on the town. (Some pizza places didn't ask a fifteen-year-old to show a license when he ordered a Pabst.) I remember Nate Mann's. The eponymous owner once fought two or three rounds with Joe Louis. Joe had a habit of crushing rope-a-dopes. When my classmates and I spoke of pizza, we didn't call it pizza. The south of Italy had its own pronunciation. We ate "ah-*beats,*" "apizza" with *b* for *p* and the last vowel omitted. I never called it pizza until I went to college.

• • •

Already I had gulped down the undistinguished food of boarding school. Each boy sat at a table of seven, and each waited on the others one day a week. At college we ate cafeteria style, so at least we had a choice, and at midnight after the beer halls closed, fuzzled, we ate at Hayes-Bickford's. Once a professor took me to the Harvard Faculty Club for lunch, where the special was horse steak, at two dollars as fulfilling as American chop suey. I've written elsewhere about my next experience in food, which was life-altering. A fellowship to Oxford acquainted me with the depths of English cooking. By the twenty-first century London's best restaurants were as good as Paris's, but not in the 1950s. An English fast-food specialty was baked beans spread on a slice of toast. "Beans on toast! Beans on toast!" we chanted as we drank warm bitter at the King's Arms. From Oxford I flew to Paris for the six-week break between terms. Food! It took an hour to fly between capitals on a propeller plane, and the airlines served lunch. I first flew to Paris on BOAC. When I flew back, I ate a garlicky snack on Air France and never considered another airline.

After Oxford, and marriage to Kirby, we spent a year at Stanford, on a fellowship of two thousand dollars a year. I remember reading ads for supermarket specials and driving all over Palo Alto to buy one item at each store, half a dollar's worth of gas to save eight cents on a package of bologna. When I heard that I had won a three-year fellowship elsewhere — to write all day — my wife and I celebrated by eating supper in Menlo Park, at a place known for its seventy-five-cent garlicky cheeseburgers.

To begin teaching at the University of Michigan I did summer school, two sections of American lit at eleven and two. I had put on weight, maybe because I ate Arby's roast beef sandwiches between meals. I dieted by taking to my office a jar for my lunch — sauerkraut, a dill pickle, and a boiled hot dog. I lost twenty pounds and gained it right back, returning to three peanut butter sandwiches midday followed by Arby's. Although I was paid a salary in Ann Arbor, my wife and children and I drank powdered milk at six cents a quart instead of the stuff that came in bottles. I was a tightwad. Otherwise we specialized in casseroles. One time Robert and Carol Bly were visiting, and Bob got mad at me for being a professor and living in a *house.* He and Carol lived in western Minnesota without electricity or water, with oil lamps and an outhouse. He pouted, and poured his beer on my supper. Calmly I picked up my plate, scraped it clean in the kitchen, and served myself more Spanish rice from the pot on the stove. When I sat back down I threw my beer in his face.

After the divorce I don't remember what I ate except for fifths of Heaven Hill, a bourbon that cost two dollars and fifty cents. My salary was nine hundred dollars a month and child support was eleven hundred, which persuaded me to write a textbook. Five years later Jane and I married. When we left Ann Arbor to move into this old house I warned her that we would have trouble finding anything to eat in New Hampshire. I talked about no fruits or vegetables out of season, no garlic, no veal cutlets, no cheese. I forgot that now we drove cars, not horses and buggies. Our market town was New London, fifteen minutes away, where our supermarket was Cricenti's. In Paris twenty-odd years earlier, I had loved *céleri rémoulade,* a starter of celery root in strips steeped in mayonnaise, mustard, vinegar, lemon juice, salt and pepper. I had never found celery root in Michigan. In the vegetable aisles of a New Hampshire grocery I found it, and also Stilton cheese, garlic, Camembert, and Bath Olivers from England. Doubtless there were Spam and sardines somewhere, but I never came across them.

For the first years here we fought over who got to cook. Jane loved to study cookbooks and I to improvise. My dishes started with garlic and a cup of olive oil, or I made meatloaf with ingenious ingredients. Once I cooked it for my daughter with three boiled quail's eggs in the middle. Another specialty of mine was beef stew with wine and onions and potatoes and garlic and basil and the rest of the spice shelf. Then my doctor told me that I had diabetes. "You mean I am pre-diabetic," I explained. "*You are diabetic,*" he told me. My disease discouraged everything that made me fat. I withdrew from the stove and Jane read diabetic cookbooks.

She loved cooking, even for a diminished eater. She specialized in unpredictable combinations brought bubbling hot to the table — steamed vegetables, mushroom sauce on cutlets. Now I cooked only for gigantic family assemblages. First I bought a huge aluminum pot. I found an old-style butcher in Tilton who corned his own beef. He dipped his metal hook into a salt barrel to lift out an honest gray joint, corned beef with no red dye. "I'd say about five pounds," he guessed as the beef dripped on the scale. Home, I would put my salt beef in the giant pot, add cabbage cut into wedges, onions, carrots, parsnips, and corn niblets, but never quail's eggs. I boiled it four hours as it disassembled into a mass that tasted of salt beef, veggies, handfuls of basil and bay leaves, and naturally garlic. At the table I carved the corned beef and added foothills of vegetables *variés*.

The aftermath of boiled dinner was better than boiled dinner. I fastened the meat grinder to the kitchen's butcher block and ground up traces of corned beef from the kettle, together with bits of cabbage and carrot and onion and anything else. The anomalous final ingredient was ground-up beets, either fresh from the garden or from Ball jars. I mashed the heap into a bowl, stirred it, and served it for breakfast or lunch or dinner or all three. This local delicacy — I haven't tasted it outside New Hampshire — is red flannel hash. I added a pinch more garlic.

Jane and I ate lunch while walking around in a daydream of bookish silence, then took a twenty-minute nap and worked all afternoon. At night Jane cooked our supper while I watched from my blue chair in the living room. She sipped a glass of white wine and I drank a beer until her voice called out, "It's ready. Come light the candles." It was the only meal at which we were formal.

The United States Information Agency stepped in and enlarged our eating experience. They sent us in 1987 for seven weeks to China and Japan to talk about American poetry. It was the longest time we spent away from our kitchen and our writing. We ate what we had never eaten, in the vastness of China ending each day with a banquet of fifty dishes, concluded by a goose. Chinese banquets nationwide began at five o'clock and ended at seven, when our hosts stood up and fled. Japan was variety — fancy city food, northern Japanese cuisine, and Korean food at a restaurant that described itself as CLEAN CLEAN CLEAN, like New Hampshire's NO GARLIC. (The Japanese had notions about foreigners' hygiene.) In Hiroshima we ate at an establishment that called it-self an Italian restaurant. It did not resemble Nate Mann's.

Later, the State Department transformed us and our culinary life. Twice they flew us to India, sending us all over the country on airplanes instead of our twenty-four-hour Chinese train rides. In such a huge country — seventeen languages and hundreds of dialects, with English the common tongue — the tastes and ingre-dients of food were vastly different across the country, from curry to yogurt, most of it Hindu and vegetarian. Cattle abounded in the streets but not on dinner plates. Jane's love for everything Hindu created our new diet. The few years left in her life, our New Hampshire kitchen became vegetarian Hindu, overflowing with spices. Once a month Jane shopped at an Indian grocery near Central Square in Cambridge. Typically she cooked one or two dishes a day, and each night assembled a new combination of food with six arms. I took to the change with enthusiasm, but whenever we went out to dinner I ate steak with garlic mashed potatoes.

Jane had leukemia for fifteen months. I don't remember what I ate in fifteen months of hospital cafeterias. Most of the time Jane ingested only TPN through a catheter in her heart. After Jane's funeral my porch filled with whole wheat bread like Jane's, cas-seroles, and a ham that I sliced for three weeks. In late spring my supper every night was fresh asparagus from the patch Jane had dug and planted and nourished across the road. Sometimes I'd buy myself two pork chops and eat one at supper with a fro-zen vegetable, two days in a row. I tried a restaurant alone, but I couldn't stand it. Only when I started dating would I eat *osso buco* again at Piero's La Meridiana. (Poetry finally attracted females, as it was supposed to do when I was fourteen.) As I escorted my date to New London's Millstone one night, the hostess asked if my companion was my granddaughter. We both shrieked "No!" and never saw the hostess again. Most of my dates were mistaken for daughters, not granddaughters. At home I made them stew with red wine. I made meatloaf. Some of them cooked in my kitchen or in theirs. A friend from California flew in bringing her own garlic press, and we bought a bushel of cloves at Cricenti's. When she took charge of the kitchen, even chocolate ice cream tasted of garlic. After my years of brief romances, I settled down with Linda. Until I stopped driving, one of us made dinner. Then we went to restaurants because I needed to get out of the house. We drove to the bookstore, the supermarket, and Piero's. He isn't reticent about cooking with garlic.

As I enter my mid-eighties my appetite dwindles. I bring home doggie bags from a restaurant. My daughter cooks me chili to freeze, and annually gives me a head of Stilton. My son keeps me supplied all year with five-year-old Vermont cheddar. Linda freezes thick soups, makes shepherd's pie and garlic potatoes. Carole gave me a quart of roadkill bear stew. Most nights I push my four-wheeled pusher to the microwave to heat up widower food. It's always Stouffer's — the red packages with Swedish Meatballs, or Stuffed Peppers, or Cheddar Potato; the white ones with Meatloaf and Potato, or Steak Portobello with Broccoli, or Ranchero Braised Beef with Sweet Potato — flakes of garlic with everything.

A House Without a Door

MY COUSIN AUDREY is ninety-six. She taught reading for sixty years, professionally and as a volunteer, at the Danbury Elementary School, which staged a celebration in her honor last fall. Audrey's mind is undiminished, but like me she walks pushing a roller with four wheels. I remarked that the school was generous to seat us together, so that she would not seem the eldest in the room. (I am eleven years younger.) I told her a recent dream in which I found myself walking in a dark house, among shadowy male strangers. I felt mildly anxious and wanted to go outside. I kept looking for a door but couldn't find one. It was a house without a door.

Audrey said, "Sometimes it's hard."

When Jane and I moved here, I worked all day on freelance writing, taking breaks between genres. For ten years, before we installed an oil furnace, I hauled wood from the shed to our centenarian cast-iron Glenwood stoves, then huffed back to my rolltop desk. With central heating I lost my trips to the woodshed.

I interrupted my work by walking our dog Gus, or by driving to browse in the Morgan Hill Bookstore, or by visiting Cricenti's to buy a jar of pimentos I didn't need. When I was eighty, after my two accidents and selling what remained of my car, it was annoying for a month not to be able to take an impulsive spin in the Honda. Gus was dead and neither the cats nor I took walks. Gradually the car desires dwindled, and I congratulated myself on accepting unavoidable limitation. Then I dreamed the dream.

My problem isn't death but old age. I fret about my lack of balance, my buckling knee, my difficulty standing up and sitting down. Yesterday I fell asleep in an armchair. I never fall asleep in a chair. Indolence overcomes me every day. I sit daydreaming about what I might do next: putting on a sweater or eating a piece of pie or calling my daughter. Sometimes I break through my daydream to stand up. At Christmas or birthday I no longer want objects, even books. I want things I can eat, cheddar or Stilton, my daughter's chili, and replacements for worn-out khakis, T-shirts, socks, and underwear. Every day in winter I wear a long-sleeved T-shirt, in summer the short-sleeved kind.

Friends die, friends become demented, friends quarrel, friends drift with old age into silence. Jane and I married in 1972, when she was twenty-four and I forty-three. For six months we delayed marriage because she would be a widow so long. After a surgeon removed half my liver, Jane wrote her elegies — "Otherwise," "Prognosis," "Pharaoh" — and the next year was crowded with generous anticipatory funerals. (A writers' group put on a Donald Hall tribute; the University of Michigan gave me an honorary degree.) I felt fine after chemo in January 1994 when Jane was diagnosed with leukemia, and in April 1995 she died. I will mourn her forever.

Ten years ago I found Linda, and she helps me get out of my house. Earlier she helped me travel, as long as a week at a time. She saw to my requirements at poetry readings from New York to Los Angeles, from the District of Columbia to Chicago, from Monterey to Pennsylvania to Kansas City. We flew to international literary festivals in Sweden, in Vancouver, in Mexico, and twice in Ireland. The places where I read my poems paid for travel, and airline credits helped us undertake more fanciful journeys. In summer we flew to temperate Argentina and Chile. May and June were right for London. July was warm enough in Russia's St. Petersburg. In spring we went to Italy, and in many seasons flew to Paris. For the first French visits we stayed at a hotel that served paradisal croissants. One morning I ate fourteen. Between one flight to Paris and another, my balance began to fail. I waddled with feet wide apart and found stairs increasingly fearsome. The entrance to our hotel was five deep steps without railings. Holly, my travel agent, found us a hotel with no stairs, only three blocks away from our old one. We clambered into taxis for museums, returning to old marvels and discovering new ones. For lunch we walked a block or two, usually to Les Deux Magots, where I ate a *sandwich Camembert,* the cheese an incomparable ripeness on a baguette warm, dense, tender, and delicious. Once the waiter took our order and shortly returned. He said it would take a few minutes; the bakery had just delivered fresh bread. How many times a day did warm baguettes arrive at Les Deux Magots? For dinner we went to fancy places — to La Tour d'Argent, to Lapérouse — but later found less notorious, more dingy and intimate restaurants. My favorite was old and plain, Joséphine "Chez Dumonet" on rue du Cherche-Midi, where they served a *boeuf bourguignon* I loved as much as the city itself.

In September of 2011 Linda and I last flew to Paris. I was eighty-three, and at home I avoided a broken hip by pushing my roller. For Paris I took only a cane, assuming that as I walked more, my legs would get stronger. Hah. After five days I moved two or three inches each step. Taxis could carry us to *boeuf bourguignon,* but I got Linda to look at paintings alone while I lay in bed reading books.

A year later Linda took a job teaching French, and over school vacation returned to France to practice the language. She went by herself.

Not everything in old age is grim. I haven't *walked* through an airport for years, and wheelchairs are the way to travel. For years a pusher has scooted me through security in fifty-four seconds, and for years I have boarded the plane before anybody else. One pusher in Minneapolis insisted that Linda sit in a wheelchair too, because Linda's walking would slow him down. He sprinted us to the luggage carousel as if he were Usain Bolt. In 2010 a university gave me an award. I flew there with Linda, and at two a.m. of the prize day I woke with stomach flu. Imodium shut me down by noon, and I struggled through my honors at four p.m. The next day I was still shaky and frail when we flew back by way of Baltimore-Washington. A pusher wheelchaired me to the Southwest Airlines gate for Manchester, New Hampshire. As usual I was first to board, Linda behind me. As we started toward the empty seats, my trousers fell down around my ankles. "Technical difficulties," Linda announced.

Poetry readings become increasingly difficult for my hosts, because I'm hard to handle — and I'm no longer doing many. My lecture agent makes sure about no stairs. If anyone says there are only a few steps, there are probably ten. (They never noticed.) Mostly I live the same day, every day, which doesn't bore me except at beginning and end. In the morning I turn on the coffee, glue in my teeth, take four pills, swallow Metamucil and wipe it off my beard, fasten a brace over my buckling knee, pull painfully tight stockings over edema — then read the newspaper and drink black coffee. Daytime is writing, napping, daydreaming, and dictating letters. Days are not boring because I read and write different things, and because writing sustains me. Bedtime is as much ennui as getting up. Fill coffee machine for morning, detach false teeth and soak them, take evening pills, remove brace, peel off painfully tight stockings.

Weeks are not boring, or months. Since I started long ago to make a living by freelance writing, it's been hard to tell day from day, week from week. Sundays the mail doesn't come. Occasionally the mail doesn't come on other days, which is puzzling until I realize it's the Fourth of July.

Old age is averse to innovation. Ten years ago I touched a computer once. It was black, it was hard, it did something weird when I touched its mouse, which was not really a mouse. I inhabit the only computerless house the length of Route 4, and I don't have an iThing. I do have a television set, for MSNBC and baseball. In newspapers and magazines I read about what's happening.

Apparently Facebook exists to extinguish friendship. E-mail and texting destroy the post office. eBay replaces garage sales. Amazon eviscerates bookstores. Technology speeds, then doubles its speed, then doubles it again. Art takes naps.

I should add that the electronically equipped Kendel lives just down the street. Like me she is handicapped, though thirty years younger. She has MS, and we compare notes on getting around. As well as typing my manuscripts and letters, she is my bookkeeper who tells me what I paid for what, and when. With my accountant she prepares my taxes. She shows me where to sign my name. If I want to know something, she finds it on Google.

When I'm annoyed by change, I think of my mother Lucy. When she could no longer live alone in her Connecticut house, Jane and I wanted her here, but she needed a medical facility. She had frequent attacks of congestive heart, which required an immediate doctor. We found her a bed in a New Hampshire place attached to a hospital, the Clough Center. Beside her was a phone jack that lacked a phone. When we bought her a telephone we found only an instrument that worked by pushbuttons, numerical as a cash register. She was disgusted. A phone has a dial!

At ninety my mother's mind remained clear. This farmhouse was twenty minutes away from her bed. She could have shuffled out of her squalid room wearing a caftan, squeezed herself into the front seat of the Honda, and sat in her childhood living room or visited the bed where she was born. She might even have smoked a cigarette. She never made the journey. In old age everything is too much trouble. The Clough Center had no door.

• • •

The ground floor of this farmhouse contains a kitchen, a bath-room, and a bedroom. I have not visited the root cellar — with its empty cider barrels, its molasses kegs, and its abandoned ping-pong table — for nearly a decade. I put in a new furnace with-out looking at it. There is a big floor upstairs with books and papers and pictures, and the workroom where Jane wrote her poems. I last climbed up — on two-hundred-year-old risers five inches deep — several years back with a man who evaluated my pictures. I use the living room for reading and writing, the par-lor for watching baseball and dictating letters. My children and grandchildren visit, which enlivens a day.

It is Carole who keeps the house. She washes my clothes, she drives me to the doctor. She arranges my furniture for comfort and safety. She examines my tick bite infection. When my bottom missed the toilet and I fell, she found and installed aluminum rails, giving me handholds. She bought an electrical chair to help me stand up. (For *some* reason, such things are easy to find sec-ondhand.) She nailed two handles to help me step on the porch. We smoke cigarettes together and I write about our habit in *Play-boy*. I depend on four women in their fifties. My trainer Pam fore-stalls the wheelchair. Linda, Kendel, and Carole do everything else. When I talk with them, I carelessly assume I'm their age, while they witness decrepitude without letting me know. I look in a mirror at my extravagant beard and I have no idea that the back of my head is bald.

When I was thirty, I lived in the future because the present was intolerable. When I was fifty and sixty, the day of love and work repeated itself year after year. Old age sits in a chair, writ-ing a little and diminishing. Exhaustion limits energy. Yesterday my first nap was at nine-thirty a.m., but when I awoke I wrote again. Some days in the evening I climb down with Linda from my porch by a stout railing and pull myself from newel post to car door to front seat. I back into the seat ass-first in order not to put my weight on a buckling knee. Linda stores my four-wheeled pusher in the trunk, so that when we arrive I can roll from the car to La Meridiana. Back home we read a novel to each other. We watch a movie from Netflix. In the morning she stirs quantities of sweet onion and five-year-old Vermont cheddar into a four-egg omelet, which is outstanding.

She leaves to teach French 4. I pick up my pen.

One feature of old age is gabbing about almost-forgotten times. I think of my great-uncle Luther, born in 1856, telling me on the farmhouse porch how he remembered the boys coming home from Virginia. I listened to a man with a white mustache who shuffled as he walked and remembered the Civil War. I was almost ten. Then New England was torn by the hurricane of 1938. Shore cottages were swept inland, power went out, houses blew down — this house survived — and in the countryside whole forests were uprooted. Roosevelt's CCC, the Civilian Conservation Corps, cut up great fallen trees and preserved the timber by corduroying lakes and ponds with logs. For many years everyone in the East reminisced about the hurricane. At some point, ten-year-old children who bicycled among freshly fallen trees will not be alive to remember the storm.

I remember the Rape of Nanking. I remember when Franco took Madrid. I remember Susan Frisbee, who lived next to Spring Glen Grammar School. I remember Frank Benedict,

Phyllis Mossberg, and Charlie Axel. I remember the Trylon and Perisphere at the 1939 World's Fair. I remember Hitler and Stalin invading Poland. I remember sitting in left field to watch the first game of the 1941 World Series. Joe Gordon hit a home run. I remember Pearl Harbor. I remember Guadalcanal. I remember buying War Bonds in school, ten cents a week. I remember leaving grammar school for the vastness of Hamden High. I remember V-E Day and Hiroshima. I remember meeting Robert Frost. I remember V-J Day and a woman's naked body. I remember Kennedy's assassination. With my son I marched in Washington against the Vietnam War. I remember 9/11. One day, of course, no one will remember what I remember.

Audrey said, "Sometimes it's hard." This farmhouse has a door, and I remember when Jane's body was carried out. I shut Gus into my workroom so that he would not see her leave.

Remains

MY GREAT-GRANDFATHER (born 1826) called our place Eagle Pond Farm because a great bald eagle lived on a hill called Eagle's Nest and fished the pond every day for its dinner. Yet his youngest child, my grandmother Kate (born 1878), never saw the bird. The land and its creatures have altered. Thirty-five years after my grandmother's death I saw a bald eagle fly over the water.

When the nineteenth century filled New Hampshire with farms, seventy percent of the state was open land. Dairy farms of forty or sixty acres lined the dirt roads, pastures for cattle behind them. When I am driven in the backcountry now, past dense forests of hardwood or soft, I see remnant stone walls that kept sheep and cattle to their allotted pastures. I see no horses, whose manure used to surface the roads. The farmers' sons and daughters deserted granite and sandy soil to work in the mills or go west where the earth was better for farming. New England has become the most forested part of the United States, eighty percent covered by trees.

In summers when I hayed with my grandfather, fewer than

half a million people lived in New Hampshire, and the land had begun its return to forest. Every quarter mile or so on Route 4 (paved 1928) a small farm—a few Holsteins with hayfields, sheep, chickens, one horse to pull or carry—struggled to survive through the labor of a farmer like my grandfather. Much land and no cash. Old backcountry farms had already returned to forest. When my grandfather and I walked in the hills, to call the cows or pick blueberries, we were wary to avoid cellar holes and abandoned wells. Sometimes we knew that a cellar hole was near because the dead farmwife's hollyhocks gave us warning. At twelve I hayed for the first time on two acres of widow hay down the road. (The farmer died; his widow wanted grass in her fields, not brush.) When Jane and I arrived, the widow's hayfield looked like virgin forest to city sorts, softwood rising high and dense. In the southern part of the state, tract houses cover the earth of old farms, and New Hampshire has more than a million people now—mainly suburbanites who live an hour or less from Boston, refugees from Taxachusetts to a state without income tax.

Dylan Thomas wrote a villanelle addressed to his father, "Do Not Go Gentle into That Good Night." The rhyming line was "Rage, rage against the dying of the light." When I met Thomas I was twenty-three and told him I loved that poem, and he told me he didn't; he said he stole it from Yeats. (Yeats in old age liked to use the word "rage.") Over the years, I've changed my mind about the poem. It showed affection and care for his father, but it asked his father to do what he could not do. In real life, a student of mine at Michigan cherished her ferocious father. He was difficult, but she had always adored his explosiveness. When he softened in age, she couldn't bear it. She spoke in something like anger, as if his weakness were willful. When Jane and I moved here, we loved a great-aunt of mine — eighty-two, younger than I am now — whose temperament was cheerful and affectionate. She and Jane spent mornings together digging dandelions, to boil the bitter leaves for dinner. My great-aunt tottered when she walked, and with difficulty climbed six cement steps, without a railing, to reach her front door. She asked her grandson, a thirty-year-old carpenter, to put up something she could hold on to. I heard him grumble, "She could climb them stairs if she was a mind to."

Everyone who practices an art should love and live with another art. One learns about one's own work by exposing oneself to a different passion. Mentioning a second art does not imply competence in practicing it. In eighth grade I flunked art, which was lamentable, because in art class I sat beside Mary Beth Burgess and I was sweet on her. Music is totally beyond me. My most notable musical moment took place on Ken Burns's *Baseball.* He interviewed me about the game, about loving baseball, not about playing it. I had hung around major league players, writing books and essays about them, and for Ken I came up with twenty anecdotes. Then he asked me to sing "Take Me Out to the Ball Game," telling me that all his interviewees would sing it. Ken Burns's charm could persuade a monkey to breed with a daffodil. At his urging I tried singing "Take me out . . ." and heard my pitch waver capriciously up and down. Tuneless, ashamed, in my disgrace I forgot the lyrics. The highlight of Ken's *Baseball* series, I swear, is the image of my mouth hanging open wide and silent. It looked like brain damage. In editing, Ken paid special attention to this image by holding it for two or three beats.

I love painting, sculpture, sketches, and watercolors. I have my own collection, mostly prints and posters — Blake, Arp, Warhol, Marie Laurencin, de Kooning, Man Ray — and my favorite pastime is going to museums. Myself, I can draw one thing only, and I do it when I sign my baseball books. I draw a circle, with half-moon semicircles inside it, with a few short lines cutting into the semicircles. The perpetually lopsided circle (I am not Giotto), decorated by expressionist stitches, leaves space for dedication, autograph, and date.

It was always poetry and not much else. To avoid math and science I took a classical diploma at Exeter — Latin and Greek, Virgil and Homer. At Harvard I majored in English but concentrated on poetry courses, avoiding prose when I could. One day, I don't know why, I wandered into the Fogg Museum and found an exhibition of Edvard Munch. I was stunned by the power of this literary painter, and I went back and back to *The Scream* and its siblings. Two years later the same show turned up in Paris, at the Petit Palais, and during a long vacation from Oxford I walked every afternoon to see it again. It began my museum life, which lasted and extended. Years later I wrote a *New Yorker* Profile of Henry Moore and interviewed other English artists, from Barbara Hepworth to Francis Bacon. I learned lots about painting and sculpture, but maybe I learned most about poetry — for instance, by hearing Moore quote Rodin, who quoted a stonemason: "Never think of a surface except as the extension of a volume."

Old houses are full of holes. A summer ago a garter snake entered and slithered across my living room. I stepped on its head and threw it outside. The same year I discovered a visitor who became my favorite for persistence. A chipmunk took up residence, and remained on the first floor for two or three months, I suppose sustained by my cat's kibble and water. Every day I would hear chirping, at first sounding like an electronic signal. Then the chipmunk came into sight, pausing with its paws tucked or folded before it. As for my cat, she stared at it intently, fascinated. Carole bought a tiny trap and baited it with whatever we imagined was a chipmunk treat. Every morning the bait was gone, but so was the chipmunk. One morning the creature skittered from the kitchen into the toolshed, where the door showed a wide space at its bottom, and never appeared again. I felt abandoned. When autumn descended into winter, I walked into the cluttered dining room, never used in old age, and smelled something rotten in a box of unsorted snapshots. Under a layer of pictures I found the small body of our chipmunk. It had not escaped after all. With a paper towel I picked it up, rigid and almost weightless, and threw it from the door as far as I could. Next morning when I opened the door to pick up the newspaper, half of his small mummified corpse lay beside the door.

At this New Hampshire house woodchucks are annoying and commonplace. Sixty years ago my cousin Freeman grew vegetables by his shack up on New Canada Road, and his shotgun took care of many such thieves. Each summer he ate one. "If they eat my peas, I'll eat *them!*" Freeman would dress the woodchuck and carry it downhill to my grandmother's woodstove. Kate held her nose as she baked it, and Freeman in his hut ate woodchuck.

Across the road from the house, my grandparents raised their year's bounty of beans, peas, onions, potatoes, and corn. The farthest part of the garden was sweet corn, which phantom raccoons ate every night. Nearer the house were peas and beans, and it was maddening to find pole beans devoured by woodchucks. When I was a boy I'd sit on a cement watering trough with my .22 Mossberg and wait for an hour to assassinate a predator. When Jane and I returned, we grew another garden. I was too impatient, nearly fifty, to sit so long with my gun. So I bought a Havahart. From the porch I could see when the trap sprung. I walked across Route 4 with the same Mossberg and killed the woodchuck trembling in my trap. Once every summer I thought of what Freeman did. In the kitchen I picked up *Joy of Cooking,* in which Irma Rombauer gives a recipe for woodchuck. When I got to the part about looking for mites when you skinned it, I closed the book and buried the corpse.

My Havahart came from an Agway, which sold farm equipment after most farmers had left. Traps were not the only solution for woodchucks. If you found a likely hole, you could try poison, but nothing worked for me except a long rifle slug from my .22. An Agway clerk told me of a customer who was especially enraged. He bought sticks of dynamite, fed them down a woodchuck hole, and blew up his whole garden.

· · ·

When I traveled with Linda to read my poems, we went to museums in city after city. At Yale we gazed into Stuart Davis's paintings and stood in front of a Schwitters collage six inches deep. In Kansas City we found large, powerful Thomas Hart Bentons. We loved Matisse everywhere. Cézanne was the better painter, but Matisse's colors overwhelmed us. We stared entranced by paintings in Paris, Rome with its ruins and the Vatican, bounteous New York, London's National Gallery and Tate, Washington, St. Petersburg and the Hermitage, Chicago with its Art Institute. In Chile we saw pre-Columbian sculpture. Pushed through museums by Linda in a wheelchair, I developed a new perspective on painting. I looked *up*. Sometimes the reflected dazzle obscured the picture, but most of the time I enjoyed my disabled angle.

Art museums in Paris, you might not expect, are generous to the handicapped. When I limped with a cane toward a long line entering the Pompidou, we were gestured to the front and admitted without charge. The last time we went there, the traveling show was Edvard Munch, of all people. Once at the Louvre we approached the *Mona Lisa,* which was encircled by a velvet cord to hold back the crowd. An attendant unfastened the cord and beckoned us inside.

Long ago I witnessed a motion from youth to age. In 1903 John Singer Sargent painted the portrait *Mrs. Fiske Warren and Her Daughter.* When I was twenty, at an occasion in Boston, I met Mrs. Fiske Warren and her daughter. I saw an old, old lady wearing a velvet choker with a cameo, her middle-aged daughter standing beside her. In Sargent's portrait from forty-odd years earlier, the mother was handsome and Bostonian, her twelve-year-old daughter leaning against her, loose-limbed and pretty and eager for the moment. The two women before me were the same and utterly altered. The daughter was plain, and looked slack or disappointed. Her mother was wrinkled and smaller, still upright in decorum and dignity, but when she spoke, her voice trembled.

Dorian Gray's portrait aged while his body stayed young.

Gray squirrels dig in the driveway. Red squirrels are sneaky and rip into insulation on the second floor, poking pink fuzzy fragments through the cracks in the toolshed's ceiling. Always there have been multitudes of mice, though not so many as when my grandfather kept a shed full of grain. Back then, a mother cat had three litters a year, and the kittens who ate mice followed my grandfather as he milked. In the tie-up he swirled a teat and sprayed Holstein milk into gaping mouths. Eventually each kitten strayed away to take a look at Route 4, and it was my chore to bury them deep enough so that something would not dig up a snack. Meanwhile the old mother dragged her teats on the barn floor and never approached the road. If mice in the house became a nuisance, my grandmother invited a cat inside for a predatory visit. Otherwise no mouse-catching cats or beloved cow-herding dogs were allowed inside. *People* lived in houses.

In 1975 Jane and I brought three cats with us from Michigan. In Ann Arbor, a town of a hundred thousand, Catto and Mia and Arabella roamed outside. New Hampshire's Route 4 turned them into house cats. They didn't seem to mind, maybe because the mouse supply was exemplary. Jane went barefoot most of the year as she walked around the house and wrote poems. She screamed a special small scream every time her bare foot squished the ripped body of a mouse, placed in her way by a cat showing off.

The small animals of 1940 remain in 2014. We see foxes, red and silver. They are handsome and seldom show themselves, but they used to be the terror of the chicken yard. Every night my grandfather shut up the hens to keep them safe. Still there are opossums playing dead or scooting around. Skunks abound. There are minks. There are fisher cats, which are not cats, but which flip porcupines over and rip open their defenseless stomachs. Undead porcupines roost high in a tree looking like birds' nests. Our dog Gus found one in a bush and came home with his muzzle sprouting quills. The vet helped out. Beavers thrive everywhere chewing down trees, and not long ago they were almost extinct. We hear of bobcats but would rather not encounter them.

There are new animals, now that the trees are back. Migrating from the west, coyotes howl all night and remain invisible. I never saw a wild turkey when I was young, walking with my grandfather. I saw my first in the 1980s. I was walking Gus when we saw a gray-feathered gobbler cross New Canada Road. Gus stood stock-still in amazement — so did I — as the turkey passed in front of us with its head bobbing. Within a year I saw in a patch of grass a gathering of twenty-five or thirty.

Deer have declined in number, although they ate my petunias last summer. Thirty-five years ago, an old orchard bloomed down the road across from a burned-out farm. Deer ate the small, wizened apples, which made the orchard handy for hunters. My uncle Everett shot a buck every year and provided deer meat for our freezer. (Never confuse deer meat, which is delicious and gamy, with a restaurant's tasteless venison.) By this time the Whittemores' orchard has disappeared under softwood. A state trooper bought the land to raise Christmas trees but never got around to it. Fewer deer, fewer hunters. My grandfather's cow pasture has grown into woods, and bear have replaced deer. Carole made bear stew. Sometimes I see an actual bear, but more often I see their scat, and when I kept a birdfeeder in the maple out front, I found a smashed birdfeeder each spring. After we had been here fifteen years, the forest increasing around us, Jane walked Gus up New Canada Road, where he treed a bear cub. If its dam had been nearby, it might have been the end of Gus, if not of Jane. Twenty years later, sometimes I see a moose, which no one saw when the land was farmed. One summer a big moose and a smaller one — I assumed a familial relationship — crossed Route 4 every morning at six, walking east from Ragged Mountain to drink from Eagle Pond. They walked with dignity under their elegant antlers, as new and as old as the returning eagle.